Certified Blockchain Expert v2

Technology Workbook

www.ipspecialist.net

Document Control

Proposal Name	:	CBE_Technology_Workbook
Document Version	:	1.0
Document Release Date	:	15th November 2018
Reference	:	CBE_WorkBook

Feedback:

If you have any comments regarding the quality of this book, or otherwise alter it to suit your needs better, you can contact us by email at info@ipspecialist.net

Please make sure to include the book title and ISBN in your message.

About IPSpecialist

IPSPECIALIST LTD. IS COMMITTED TO EXCELLENCE AND DEDICATED TO YOUR SUCCESS.

Our philosophy is to treat our customers like family. We want you to succeed, and we are willing to do anything possible to help you make it happen. We have the proof to back up our claims. We strive to accelerate billions of careers with great courses, accessibility, and affordability. We believe that continuous learning and knowledge evolutions are the most important things to keep re-skilling and up-skilling the world.

Planning and creating a specific goal is where IPSpecialist helps. We can create a career track that suits your visions as well as develop the competencies you need to become a professional Network Engineer. We can also assist you with the execution and evaluation of proficiency level based on the career track you choose, as they are customized to fit your specific goals.

We help you STAND OUT from the crowd through our detailed IP training content packages.

Course Features:

- · Self-Paced learning
- O Learn at your own pace and in your own time
- · Covers Complete Exam Blueprint
- O Prep-up for the exam with confidence
- · Case Study Based Learning
- O Relate the content to real-life scenarios
- · Subscriptions that suits you
- O Get more and pay less with IPS Subscriptions
- · Career Advisory Services
- O Let industry experts plan your career journey
- · Virtual Labs to test your skills
- O With IPS vRacks, you can testify your exam preparations
- · Practice Questions
- O Practice questions to measure your preparation standards
- · On Request Digital Certification
- O On request, digital certification from IPSpecialist LTD.

About the Authors:

This book has been compiled with the help of multiple professional engineers. These engineers specialize in different fields e.g. Networking, Security, Cloud, Big Data, IoT etc. Each engineer develops content in its specialized field that is compiled to form a comprehensive certification guide.

About the Technical Reviewers:

Nouman Ahmed Khan

AWS-Architect, CCDE, CCIEX5 (R&S, SP, Security, DC, Wireless), CISSP, CISA, CISM is a Solution Architect working with a major telecommunication provider in Qatar. He works with enterprises, mega-projects, and service providers to help them select the best-fit technology solutions. He also works closely as a consultant to understand customer business processes and helps select an appropriate technology strategy to support business goals. He has more than 14 years of experience working in Pakistan/Middle-East & the UK. He holds a Bachelor of Engineering Degree from NED University, Pakistan, and M.Sc. in Computer Networks from the UK.

Abubakar Saeed

Abubakar Saeed has more than twenty-five years of experience in managing, consulting, designing, and implementing large-scale technology projects, extensive experience heading ISP operations, solutions integration, heading Product Development, Presales, and Solution Design. Emphasizing on adhering to Project timelines and delivering as per customer expectations, he always leads the project in the right direction with his innovative ideas and excellent management.

Muhammad Yousuf

Muhammad Yousuf is a professional technical content writer. He is Cisco Certified Network Associate in Routing and Switching. He holds a bachelor's degree in Telecommunication, Engineering from Sir Syed University of Engineering and Technology. He has both technical knowledge and industry sounding information, which he uses perfectly in his career.

Farah Qadir

Farah Qadir is a professional technical content writer, holding bachelor's degree in Telecommunication Engineering from Sir Syed University of Engineering and Technology. With strong educational background, she possesses exceptional researching and writing skills that has led her to impart knowledge through her professional career.

Muhammad Khawar

Muhammad Khawar is a professional technical content writer. He holds a bachelor's degree in Computer Science from Virtual University of Pakistan. He was working as an IT Executive in a reputable organization. He has completed training of CCNA Routing and Switching, .NET and Web designing. He as both technical knowledge and industry sounding information.

Free Resources:

With each workbook you buy from Amazon, IPSpecialist offers free resources to our valuable customers.

Once you buy this book, you will have to contact us at info@ipspecialist.net to get this limited time offer without any extra charge.

Free Resources Include:

Exam Practice Questions in Quiz Simulation: IP Specialists' Practice Questions have been developed keeping in mind the certification exam perspective. The collection of these questions from our technology workbooks is prepared to keep the exam blueprint in mind, covering not only important but necessary topics as well. It is an ideal document to practice and revise your certification.

Career Report: This report is a step by step guide for a novice who wants to develop his/her career in the field of computer networks. It answers the following queries:

- Current scenarios and future prospects.
- Is this industry moving towards saturation or are new opportunities knocking at the door?

- What will the monetary benefits be?
- Why get certified?
- How to plan and when will I complete the certifications if I start today?
- Is there any career track that I can follow to accomplish specialization level?

Furthermore, this guide provides a comprehensive career path towards being a specialist in the field of networking and also highlights the tracks needed to obtain certification.

IPS Personalized Technical Support for Customers: Good customer service means helping customers efficiently, in a friendly manner. It is essential to be able to handle issues for customers and do your best to ensure they are satisfied. Providing good service is one of the most important things that can set our business apart from the others of its kind.

Great customer service will result in attracting more customers and attain maximum customer retention.

IPS is offering personalized TECH support to its customers to provide better value for money. If you have any queries related to technology and labs you can simply ask our technical team for assistance via Live Chat or Email.

Our Products

Technology Workbooks

IPSpecialist Technology workbooks are the ideal guides to developing the hands-on skills necessary to pass the exam. Our workbook covers official exam blueprint and explains the technology with real life case study based labs. The content covered in each workbook consists of individually focused technology topics presented in an easy-to-follow, goal-oriented, step-by-step approach. Every scenario features detailed breakdowns and thorough verifications to help you completely understand the task and associated technology.

We extensively used mind maps in our workbooks to visually explain the technology. Our workbooks have become a widely used tool to learn and remember the information effectively.

Quick Reference Sheets

Our quick reference sheets are a concise bundling of condensed notes of the complete exam blueprint for Certified Blockchain Expert CBEv2. It's an ideal handy document to help you remember the most important technology concepts related to CBEv2 exam.

Practice Questions

IP Specialists' Practice Questions are dedicatedly designed for certification exam perspective. The collection of these questions from our technology workbooks are prepared to keep the exam blueprint in mind covering not only important but necessary topics as well. It's an ideal document to practice and revise your certification.

IPS Personalized Technical Support for Customers: Good customer service means helping customers efficiently, in a friendly manner. It is essential to be able to handle issues for customers and do your best to ensure they are satisfied. Providing good service is one of the most important things that can set our business apart from the others of its kind.

Great customer service will result in attracting more customers and attain maximum customer retention.

IPS is offering personalized TECH support to its customers to provide better value for money. If you have any queries related to technology and labs you can simply ask our technical team for assistance via Live Chat or Email.

Become an author & earn with us: If you are interested in becoming an author and start earning passive income, IPSpecialist offers "Earn with us" program. We all consume, develop and create content during our learning process, certification exam preparations, and during searching, developing and refining our professional careers. That content, notes, guides, worksheets and flip cards among other material is normally for our own reference without any defined structure or special considerations required for formal publishing.

IPSpecialist can help you craft this 'draft' content into a fine product with the help of our global team of experts. We sell your content via different channels as:

1. Amazon – Kindle
2. eBay
3. LuLu

4. Kobo
5. Google Books
6. Udemy and many 3rd party publishers and resellers

Contents at a glance

Table of Contents

About this Workbook

This workbook covers all the information you need to pass the Blockchain Council's *Certified Blockchain Expert v2* exam. The workbook is designed to deliver all information and technical knowledge in-depth for learning with real-life examples and case studies.

➢ Covers complete blueprint
➢ Detailed content
➢ Case Study based approach
➢ Pass guarantee
➢ Mind maps

About the Certified Blockchain Expert v2 Exam

Length of exam:	1 hour
Number of questions:	100
Question format:	Multiple choice
Passing grade:	60%
Exam language availability:	French, German, Brazilian Portuguese, Spanish, Japanese, Simplified Chinese, Korean
Testing centre:	Training & Exam both will be online at Tosh Academy

A Certified Blockchain Expert is a skilled professional who understands and knows deeply what Blockchain is and how Blockchain works, it uses the same knowledge to build Blockchain-based applications for enterprises and businesses. The CBE credential certifies individuals in the Blockchain discipline of Distributed Ledger Technology from a vendor-neutral perspective.

Certified Blockchain Professional is an exhaustive training, lab & exam based program aim to provide a proof of the knowledge of the certificate holder in Blockchain space. The blockchain is evolving very fast & enabling businesses to build powerful solutions at a lesser cost. Enterprises are struggling to identify the right talent to deploy on the Blockchain-based projects in-house. This certification will work as a bridge between enterprises &

resources (employees, consultants & advisors) to give enterprises confidence in the quick hire.

Who must attend this certificate?

- Investment Banker, Consultant & Advisors
- University Professors
- Engineering & Management Students
- Programmers & Developers
- Software Engineers & Architects
- Application Architects
- Cryptocurrency Enthusiasts
- CEO, CTO, CIO, CISO or any other CXO
- Operations Head in Businesses
- Senior Government Officials
- Security Professionals, Administrators
- Venture Capitalists, Angel & Seed Investors

Benefits:

- Get job assistance
- Prove your Blockchain skills & understanding
- Grasp the deep understanding of Blockchain & how it works
- Implement your skills in any Blockchain projects
- Build your own Blockchain businesses with acquired knowledge

Requirements:

- Basic knowledge of Computer Science
- Awareness of Cryptocurrencies like Bitcoin, Ethereum etc.
- Must be motivated enough to learn blockchain deeply

Experience required:

There are no such recommended experience required for getting this certification

The purpose of the CBE credential is to:

- Establish and govern minimum standards for credentialing professional Blockchain.
- Inform the public that credentialed individuals meet or exceed the minimum standards.

Reinforce Blockchain expertise as a unique and self-regulating profession.

Chapter 01: Block Chain Basics

Blockchain Technology

The Blockchain technology is a concept of the distributed ledger or P2P (Peer-to-peer) shared ledger on a peer-to-peer network. A blockchain is a chain of blocks stored on the hundreds and thousands of computers across the globe and distributed over the geographical location. In blockchain technology, digital information is distributed among peers all over the world; this information is distributed among thousands of machines, not stored at any single location, all records are public and easily verifiable. It is a complete ledger that keeps the copy of all the credits or debits of digital assets. That digital assets can be a bank transaction statement, digital currency or any digital information. For example, consider a bank statement of several transactions. These transactions are recorded into a chain of blocks. This chain of blocks is distributed among thousands of peers across the globe so that each peer can individually verify the transaction without involving any other peer.

The blockchain technology is using decentralized network architecture to maintain its network, it means, block chaining is not centrally controlled by any corporation or agency but a decentralized network to make it more secure. According to Block Chain Council, the term "**Blockchain technology**" typically refers to the transparent, trustless, publicly accessible ledger that allows us to securely transfer the ownership of units of value using public key encryption and proof of work methods.

The term *Trustless* is popularly used with blockchain technology. It does not eliminate the trust between the peers, but reduces the level of trust required required from each entity in the system. To make it trustless, trust is distributed among different actors. These actors are the miners, who put computational power to maintain and secure the ledger. The more miners in a network, the more resources are shared hence, the network is more secured.

Therefore, the blockchain is decentralized ledger tracking digital assets on the P2P network. When we sayP2P network, it means peer-to-peer or decentralized network, where all the computers are connected in some way, and each computer holds the complete copy of the ledger.

Consider a bank account having transactions on a daily basis. The full ledger will keep track of every transactional amount either credit or debit. When the account holder demands the complete balance statement from the bank, the statement contains every transaction

record with a time stamp. You can validate the transactions from the balance statement. Similarly, each block records the transactions. As we known, every new block is connected with the previous block so that the entire blockchain will contain the total number of transactions from the beginning.

Centralized network:

The centralizednetwork always has a central root node or a root server that connects to all child nodes and always keeps the control inside. In a centralized network, all users and end-point devices are connected with a single, central node that controls all nodes and all communication throughout the network. The centralized network offers better controlling and visibility over the network, dependency regarding single-point of failure, and no data or application redundancy.

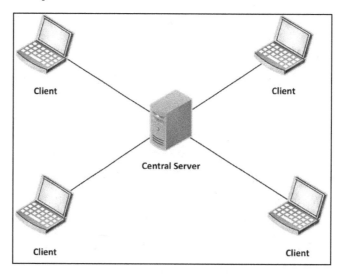

Figure 1-01: Centralized Network

Decentralized Network:

Decentralized networks are being distributed among multiple nodes however a decentralized network may be either distributed or a point-to-point network. There is no centralized node controlling the entire network as a single point of control, it can be multiple or more than one node.

Distributed Network:

Distributed networks are comprised of multiple central nodes, connected and controlling several sub-nodes or endpoints. Distributed networks have divided control over the network among root nodes.

Distributed networks or P2P networks are categorized in the decentralized network because both of these networks have divided control. In a P2P network, the system that includes each node is connected to the other node directly or indirectly.

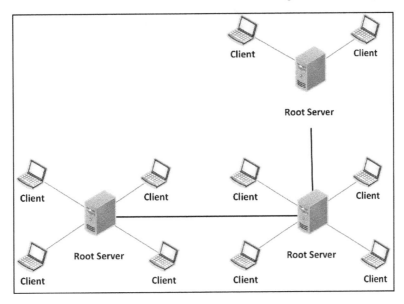

Figure 1-02: Distributed Network

Peer-to-peer network is another type of decentralized network where peers are referred as computer systems or endpoint devices connected and sharing resources with another peer via internet without the need of central or root server. Each endpoint acts as a file server or client to communicate over the P2P network. Sender of the file will become server whereas receiver of the file will be client.

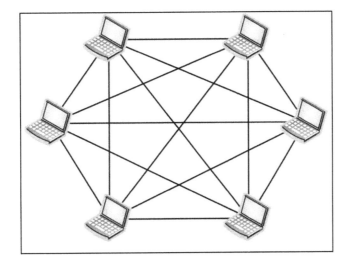

Figure 1-03: Peer-to-Peer Network Model

The difference between client/server model and peer-to-peer network is very common. Peer-to-peer network, as defined above, requires no central server to communicate or share resources with the remote peer over the internet. Whereas, in a client server model, resources are shared over the server and can be accessible by any client. The client has to provide username and password to authenticate themselves, thus the client/server model possesses more security than a peer-to-peer network.

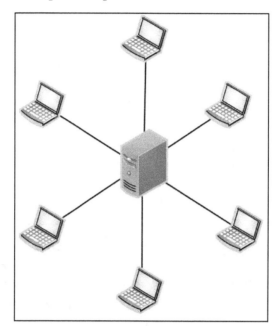

Figure 1-04: Client-Server Model

Block chaining is the technology that works on a P2P network for a distributed ledger. This distributed ledger includes information about digital assets. Therefore, the blockchain is a ledger that stores the credit or debit of every single record in such away that it cannot be tampered by anyone without letting the other notice in the changing or tampering. Every block and page are connected to each other. In a way, blockchain is related to cryptocurrencies but is not a cryptocurrency.

How Block Chaining Works?

To understand the operation or workflow of block chaining, consider some transactions among three clients namely, A, B and C. First block of the chain is called "*Genesis block*." Genesis block may also be called "Block 0" or "Day-Zero Block." Each client initially has some balance amount, for example, client A has five coins, client B also has five coins, whereas client C has tencoins. *The nonce* is a 32-bit random or pseudo-random arbitrary number assigned by the miner to each block to ensure old communication is not replayed.

Furthermore, it can be used as an initialization vector and in cryptographic hashing functions.

Sign n -1 value for genesis block is 0, because ***sign n*** denotes the hash value of the previous block which is none for the case of genesis block. When we move to block 1, sign n value will be considered for block 1 will be the hash value of the previous block (block 0), and so on.

Furthermore, genesis block contains some transactions, as shown in the figure below:

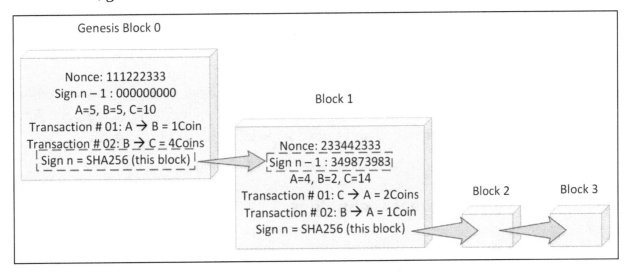

Figure 1-05: Block Chaining Process

In genesis block, as shown in figure 1-05, user A transferred one coin to user B. Similarly, user B transferred four coins to user C. Now, user A has four coins, user B has two coins, and user C has coins. Now the hash value is calculated for this block (genesis block) using the SHA-256 algorithm to ensure the integrity of the block.

Now, moving to block 1, "*Nonce*" value and "*Sign n -1*" value is to be calculated for this block. Sign n -1 value will require the SHA-256 value of the previous block (Block 0). Transactions are saved in this block in the same way as for previous block. At last, SHA-256 value is calculated for this block and in the same way, the chain continues.

Why is Blockchain Essential?

The blockchain is an interesting technology that underpins the digital currency bitcoin. Bitcoin has a main application and is commercialized in a growing number of areas and the public sector to which it opens up its financial services.

What is the reason behind the blockchain?

The purpose of blockchain is to establish and govern minimum standards, to develope measurements and inform the public if the individual meets or exceeds the minimum standard. Being a blockchain expert is a unique and self-regulating profession.

This certification is well suited for an investment banker, consultant, and advisors who are advising a company in the blockchain space or in the supply chain health care. It is for those who are looking to understand blockchain and how it can be used. The certification is also suited for university professors, engineering and management students, programmers and developers, security professionals, administrators, senior government officials and operation heads in businesses.

In today's modern era, blockchain experts are highly valued. Many organizations are looking for a certified blockchain expert and certified blockchain developers. This certification is the basic understood and gained knowledge of the blockchain.

You can build your own blockchain business with the acquired knowledge.

Blockchain Vs Traditional Technology

The blockchain is completely different from traditional technology. In the blockchain database, each participant maintains updates and calculates the new entries into a database, all nodes work together.

In a traditional database, running on the internet utilizes client-server network architecture. It means, clients can change entries that are present in the centralized server.

Blockchain Database	Traditional Database
Decentralized control: it allows different parties who do not know each other but share information without needing a central system.	Centralized control: it is controlled by the administrator.
History of record	No history of record
There is no confidentiality of information; information on blockchain is public.	In traditional databases, information is accessible by authorized member.
No Access Control is required	Requires Access Control
There are two functions of the blockchain	There are four functions of traditional

▪ Read ▪ Write	▪ Create ▪ Read ▪ Update ▪ Delete

Table 1-01: Difference between blockchain and traditional database

Table 1-01 helps us in gaining a better understanding of the differences between the functions of the blockchain and that of the traditional database.

Benefits of using blockchain technology:

Lack of Trust

The most important advantage of blockchain technology is a trustless system. In a typical system, you have to trust different entities within a system such as users, administrators, third parties and others. If any of the trusted party is compromised, the entire system becomes vulnerable.

Trustless nature of blockchain technology eliminates the need of trusting any entity within a system. When you are relying on a decentralized-ledger, you have distributed the trust among several miners who are responsible to compute validate and compare the transactions to keep it secure. You do not have to trust anyone to trust the ledger's data. All blockchain-based ledgers are maintained by multiple nodes through the consensus-based algorithm.

Availability

How available is the blockchain system?

- It is a decentralized system.
- It is nearly impossible to shut down all nodes distributed all over the world at the same time.

Verifiability and Auditability

- Any record of transaction can be verified by anyone openly whether it is running on a public or private blockchain based ledger with the permission.
- Auditability or verifiability does not mean the records are always accessible. There can be encryption layers on top of it, matching the record tape for security.

- It is easy to audit any transaction & the trail of it. This becomes a much more meaningful talk about the regulators. To know the business or use cases when the regulator is needed to audit the perfect usage.

The Immutable ledger of Transparency

Another most important thing that blockchain offers is an immutable ledger. This has been a standout amongst the most praised highlights of relatively every blockchain.

- Essentially, immutability is the most trusted for having the capacity to detect and prevent 'double sending.' 'If everyone trusts the ledger's content to be immutable, prevention of double sending would be at any rate exceptionally faulty and virtually impossible.
- The blockchain is purposefully made to be practically immutable, i.e., no one (in theory, at least) can alter the blockchain's 'distributed ledger' of every single committed block.
- Bitcoin or Ehtereum is the most popular implementation of the blockchain; immutability is accomplished by means of 'proof of work' system. It is the integral and the required part of their consensus reaching algorithm.

What is "Proof of Work"?

Proof-of-work is basically a consensus algorithm used in blockchain technology that proves the transactions and adds new blocks in the existing blockchain. Computation of PoW i.e. solving the mathematical puzzle is a difficult operation in terms of time consumption and resources required to compute, however it is easy to validate.

The responsible entities in a network are called **Miners** whereas the process is called **Mining**.

PoW is basically a competition among miners to complete the process of pending transaction in order to confirm & verify the transactions and to produce a new block in the existing blockchain. Miners are rewarded for the PoW and for bearing this responsibility.

High security

Blockchain, hence is a decentralized track, as a result, the blockchain follows the longest chain rule.

Longest chain rule

- This means that all the nodes will always follow the longest chain. To handle a conflict in the blockchain, longest chain rule is applied. In case where two or more miners build the block simultaneously, the longest chain will continue the blocks whereas other chains will be discarded. Longest chain rule is defined in next chapter in detail.

Computational Expensive

The mining process in a blockchain requires heavy computational resources. Heavy hardware is required for mining. Comparing to a centralized system, computation resources required in a blockchain technology and time consumption is always slower than a centralized network.

Decentralized Nature

The blockchain is more secured because of its' decentralized nature.

- There are many honest nodes in the network. Corrupting anyone in the network at the same time is literally not possible.
- Faking the transaction is impossible since the other honest nodes can easily identify and reject the transaction.
- The blockchain is more secure if the proof of work is high.

Faster dealing and cost saving

Few application relating to financial services of blockchain are as follows;

- Capital market
- Trade services
- Investment
- Payment
- Wealth management
- Securities
- Commodities exchanges

One of the main advantage of the blockchain technology is the goal of cost saving. Distributed ledger technology can easily reduce the financial services' cost between US $15 billions and $20 billion per annum. It is possible to provide decommissions in the legacy system and significantly reduce IT costs. It also operates a lot quicker as well.

What are the different Blockchain Technologies?

Bitcoin

Bitcoin is an application of blockchain and implementation of the blockchain. Bitcoin is the cryptocurrency whose ledger is maintained by the blockchain openly.

The concept of "Proof of work" is to build a bitcoin platform where the data produced is expensive and time-intensive. In the case of bitcoin, proof of work is making through the process of "mining."

The transactions are connected to the bitcoin user's address that is stored on a general ledger called blockchain.

Figure 1-06: Bitcoin

Ethereum

Another application of blockchain is Ethereum launched on 30[th]july 2015. Ethereum is a platform to build decentralization applications revolving around the smart contract execution platform where we can deploy the smart contract and execute them.

Ethereum is the currency or token that is fuelling the entire network. Proof of Work and Proof of Stake consensus algorithms are used in Ethereum to validate transactions.

Figure 1-07: Ethereum

Visit the website https://etherscan.io to check Ethereum blocks.

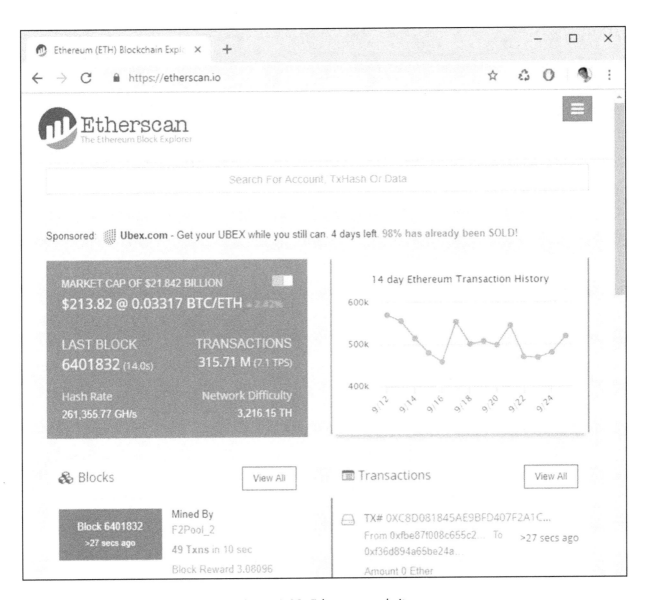

Figure 1-08: Ethereum website

Smart contract

Smart contract is used to define the computer program code that is capable of facilitating, executing and enforcing the negotiation or the performance of an agreement by using blockchain technology. There is also a smart program that runs on the blockchain.

Multichain

Multi-chain is another platform to establish the private blockchain. Multi-chain provides an API and command-line interface for setup. In multi-chain, the transaction fees and the block incentive is null by default. Hand-shaking process in Multi-chain helps to identify two nodes representing themselves with an address and list of permissions. The mining process of multi-chain is defined in a criterion known as *"Mining diversity"*.

Recordkeeper

Recordkeeper is an open, public blockchain to keep your records. Recordskeeper's public blokchain allows you to create verfiable and immutale records of any types of data which is not possible in traditional technologies like MySQL, Oracle and MSSQL.

Recordkeeper is a public chain for record keeping and data security. It also allows the users to retrieve the uploaded data by using the key. Data upload is calculated as per the data's size or by the cost.

It is an open source platform for private blockchain that offers a set of key points including:

- Rapid deployment
- Configurability
- Data stream
- Permission management

Hyperledger

Hyperledger is an open sourced community of communities that benefits an ecosystem of hyperledger based solution providers and users.-It focuses on the blockchain related use case that cross a variety of industrial sectors.

What the reason behind creating hyperledger:

- We know that a blockchain is a P2P distributed ledger forged by consent, joined with a system for smart contract and other useful technologies. Together they help in building a new gensis of transactional functions.
- It acts as an operating system for a data-sharing network, micro-currencies, marketplace, and decentralized digital communications.
- It conducts business processes and legal constraints, these functions establish accountability, trust, and transparency at the core.
- This includes various blockchains with their own particular consent and storage models and services for identity, access control and contracts.

NEO

- NEO is similar to the ethereum. NEO runs the decentralized software. The difference of the NEO is that NEO is written in a programming language like Python. While the main focus of NEO is on a smart economy, ethereum blockchain focuses on a smart contract.
- NEO lets clients digitize certain assets and track them on its blockchain. Making it easier to trade on them as the client sees fit.

Figure 1-09: NEO

Stellar

- Stellar is an open source or distributed. It is the network of the decentralized server. A complete copy of global ledger exists on each stellar.
- The ledger records each transaction of the system for the companies and people alike. It records your money as credits that are issued by Anchors. This acts as a bridge between given currencies and stellar of the network.
- Stellar does not manage all type of software like ethereum. ICO aside is not the choice of ethereum.
- Stellar can manage exchanges between cryptocurrencies and fit-based currencies, like a ripple.

The network becomes stronger as the number of people running on these nodes increases.

Figure 1-10: Stellar

EOS

EOS is the one of the most or the newest blockchain technology to enter the cryptocurrency network. EOS blockchain is aiming to build a decentralized operating system that can process fast and free transactions. It's ICO (Initial Coin Offering) has been interesting for a couple of reasons. ICO is a kind of funding using cryptocurrencies.

EOS offers the solutions at enterprise level such as Smart contracts, dApps (decentralized applications) hosting and decentralized storage. EOS sees the solution to solve the problems of usability. Such as, steam and bitshares can process around transaction per second and use smart contract technology. It is very difficult for developers to insert basic functions.

EOS is referred as "Ethereum killer." Both ethereum and EOS are capable of hosting dApps; the smart contract is supported by both of them. The difference is the amount of transaction each network can process at a given time.

Ethereum is only able to process about 15 transactions in every second, but EOS is hoping to increase this number over millions. Perhaps EOS could be the real Ethereum killer.

Blockchain Ecosystem

Blockchain ecosystem refers different entities within a blockchain system and their interactions with each other such as users, miners, developers, exchanges and applications and the rest of the internet user. Following are some important stakeholders of blockchain ecosystem:

1. Users
2. Developers
3. Miners
4. Exchanges

Blockchain developers

Blockchain developers are those who design, implement and support a blockchain network. Basically, blockchain developers develop using blockchain technology.People settling around the architecture and designing models of blockchain are called blockchain developers.

Types of blockchain developer

There are two types of blockchain developer;

- Blockchain core developer
- Blockchain software developer

Blockchain core developer

Blockchain core developer works on the design architecture of the blockchain network.

They are similar to the blockchain web developers who have included the development protocols like STTP, SLL, and network on architecture.

Role of blockchain core developer

The main role of blockchain core developer is as follows:

- Manage the architecture network
- Supervise the blockchain network
- Work on census algorithm
- Setup blockchain protocol

Blockchain software developer

Blockchain software developer works on the blockchain to create applications.

Role of blockchain software developer

The main role of blockchain software developer is as follows:

- Create a smart contract
- Develop a distributed app
- Work on front and back-end application development
- Supervision of full stack

How do you became a blockchain developer?

We should know the technical knowledge like

- Understanding the blockchain architecture
- Understanding the data structures
- Understanding the basic principles of cryptography used in the blockchain
- Learn languages used for smart contract development
- Basics of web-development

Blockchain Miners

Mining

The process of recording the pending transaction by adding a new block into the blockchain through mathematical puzzle (proof of work) is called blockchain mining.

What are the miners?

Miners are referred to a computer or server that does all the required computation to guess a new block.

How does it work?

Miner uses CPU power to identify the random number through which they create a digest or signature of the next block. In such away that the new signature is in a particular order; it can be larger than the previous block or it can have some other logic, but it has to be particular in a systematic way.

In such a way, a new signature is lesser than the previous digest. This means the whole change can be described in a descending order, or it can be in an ascending order, depending on the blockchain that is using it. To calculate this hash, the miner submits the hash to the network and waits for a response. Submitting the hash does not mean that they will get an approval. Their block can also be rejected. Hence, the signature of the new block must be less than the recently added blocks.

Miners do this first, then announce it to the entire network and get the benefits.

Blockchain Applications

Blockchain ecosystem application is considered to be the developer of communities and businesses that can be built to create their own particular services and projects.

As we know, the applications of blockchain are:

- Ethereum
- NEO
- Stellar

Ethereum

Basically, ethereum is the application of blockchain which has three kinds of applications;

- Financial application
- Semi-financial application

- Non financial application

Financial application

Financial application gives users strong ways of managing and entering into contracts using money. This includes financial derivatives, hedging contracts, sub-currencies, saving wallets and even instruments like employment contracts.

Semi-financial Application

Semi-financial application involves money, although there is also a heavy non-monetary side.

Nonfinancial Application

Nonfinancial application includes applications such as online voting and governance mechanism. Basically, this is not financial at all.

NEO

NEO is one of the most popular applications of blockchain ecosystem. There are the benefits of NEO ecosystem that invest in upcoming projects. Developers create their own particular alliances such as NEO's city of Zions. It also helps to create or build infrastructure projects for NEO. NEO has NGC (NEO global capital).

Stellar

Another application of the blockchain ecosystem is stellar. Stellars have two main components; first one is that user is running stellar nodes on their machines. The second one is the conversion of cryptocurrency to fiat currency.

Blockchain Exchanges

Each blockchain project has an ecosystem that includes a decentralized exchange. This may be developed by a developer, project team or community.

There are some exchanges as follows:

- Stellar's SDEX exchange
- NEO'S NEX exchange
- EtherDelta

Stellar's SDEX Exchanges

Stellar SDEX is the working name for the project,and internal prototypes are underway. It is designed to find the rates between two digital assets, making it trade crypto. It will enable a chain, protocol-level trades and minimize spread and maximize the choice of assets.

Stellar is the major exchange. It will need to increase the quality and numbers of anchors and market-makers on our network.

Some points of SDEX include:

- Very low trading fees
- End-user control of secret keys
- Trading for stellar ICO tokens

Lighting network on stellar:

According to Stellar, "Lightning is a scaling solution for distributed payment networks, originally proposed for the Bitcoin blockchain. Lightning is designed to allow users to make off-chain payments through routers and hubs. Lightning even has the potential to support cross-protocol payments, such as a payment where the sender sends Bitcoins on the Bitcoin network and the recipient receives lumens on the Stellar network, without having to trust any parties in between."

NEO's NEX Exchanges

NEX is a platform that merges blockchain with the off-chain matching engine to enable faster and more complex trades.

NEX has some components that are as follows;

- **High volume:** NEX manages trade volume through the off-chain matching engine.
- **Payment services:** It enables smart contract on NEO to send and receive global assets.
- **Complex trades:** NEX manages complex order type that is not currently available on the decentralized exchange.
- **NEX wallet extension**: This underpins the NEX ecosystem, allowing fast and seamless coordinate between NEX, dApps, and websites.
- **Cross-chain trading:** NEX allows performing at nodes between token based on NEO and ethereum.

EtherDelta

EtherDelta is one of the decentralized exchange that is used for trading ethereum token. For example, the user can create a wallet directly on the site.

Blockchain Vs Bitcoin

Blockchain

Blockchain was invented by Satoshi Nakamoto in 2008. The blockchain is a technology that has the concept of the distributed ledger or P2P shared on a P2P network. The blockchain is decentralized ledger tracking digital assets on the P2P network.

What about bitcoin?

Bitcoin is the crypto-currency application which deals in digital currency (BTC) only. The transactions are connected to the user's bitcoin address, stored in a general ledger. The digital number that is being tracked in the ledger is called Bitcoin.

The concept of "Proof of work" is to build a bitcoin platform where data produced is expensive and time-intensive. In the case of bitcoin, proof of work is making through the process of "mining."

Bitcoin	Blockchain
Bitcoin is a crypto-currency.	Blockchain is a decentralized ledger
It focuses to speed-up cross-border transactions and reduces the governmental control.	It is decentralized ledger which keep the records of all peer to peer transaction.
Bitcoin application is limited to trading digital currency	Blockchain can easily trade with currencies to property rights
Limited application	Blockchain is open, having vast scope in supply chain, health care, smart contract and other domains.

Table 1-02: Difference between blockchain and bitcoin

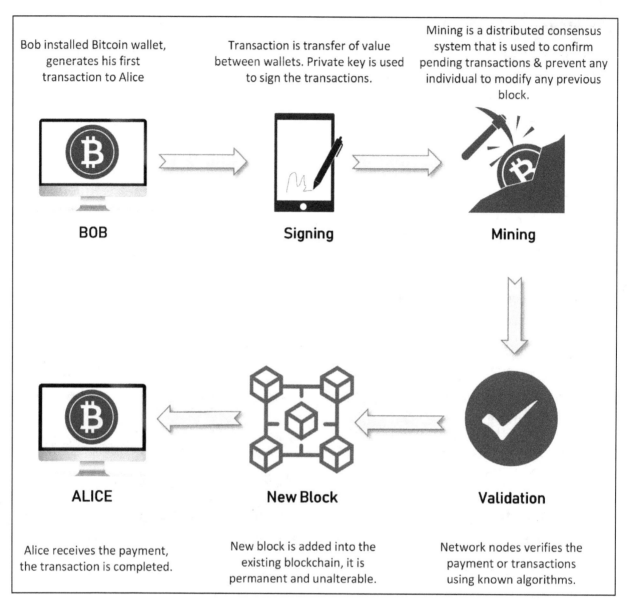

Figure 1-11: How the Bitcoin works

1. Above figure shows, Bob generates his first transaction to Alice. Using his wallet, bob sends the bitcoin to Alice's address.
2. Private key signs the transaction to confirm the authenticity of the source.
3. Miners in the network compute the pending transaction and calculating the hashes. The first correct miner will get rewarded for this mining.
4. Nodes within the network validate the transaction.
5. If the transaction is verified, new block is added in the existing blockchain. This newly added block is secured from being altered.

6. Upon successful addition of new block, payment is transferred to Alice's wallet.

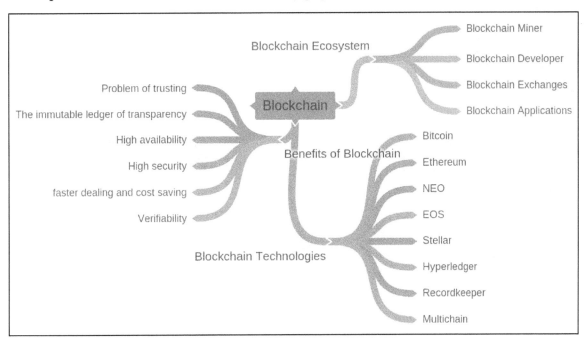

Practice Questions:

1. Who invented blockchain?
   A. Leaonhar Euler
   B. Issac Newton
   C. Amedeo Avograado
   D. Satoshi Nakamoto

2. What is blockchain?
   A. It is a technology
   B. It is a concept
   C. It is an implementation
   D. It is an application

3. Which one of the following is a decentralized ledger tracking digital assets on the P2P network?
   A. Bitcoin
   B. Blockchain
   C. Ethereum
   D. None of the above

4. Which nodes are being distributed among the multiple nodes?
   A. Centralized network
   B. Distributed network
   C. Decentralized network
   D. All of the above

5. What is bitcoin?
   A. It is an application
   B. It is an implementation
   C. It is a cryptocurrency
   D. All of the above

6. The transactions are connected to the user's bitcoin address that is stored on a general ledger is called?
   A. Bitcoin
   B. Ethereum
   C. Blockchain
   D. Ripple

7. Which concept is used to build a bitcoin platform?
   A. Proof of state
   B. Proof of work
   C. Mining
   D. None of the above

8. Bitcoin is equal to?
   A. Unicorn

   B. Toy silver unicorn
   C. Toy golden unicorn
   D. All of the above

9. Which about the following statement is used to define the computer program code that is capable of the facilitating, executing and enforcing the negotiation or the performance of an agreement by using blockchain technology?
   A. Proof of work
   B. Smart contract
   C. Cryptocurrency
   D. Proof of state

10. What are the benefits of using blockchain technology?
    A. High security
    B. High availability
    C. Verifiability and auditability
    D. Trustless

11. What are the applications of cost saving and faster dealing?
    A. Trade services
    B. Investment
    C. Payment
    D. Wealth management
    E. Securities

12. How many functions of blockchain database are there? Name them.
    A. 2
    B. 3
    C. 4
    D. 5

13. How many functions of the traditional database are there? Name them.
    A. 3
    B. 4

C. 5

D. 6

14. What is the process of recording the pending transaction by adding a new block into the blockchain through mathematical puzzle (proof of work) called?
A. Blockchain miner
B. Blockchain mining
C. Bitcoin
D. None of the above

15. What is a miner?
A. The process of recording the pending transaction by adding a new block into the blockchain through mathematical puzzle (proof of work).
B. Those who are referred to as computer or server that does all the required computation to guess a new block.
C. None of the above

16. What are the applications of blockchain?
A. Bitcoin
B. Ethereum
C. NEO
D. All of the above

17. How many types of blockchain developer are there? Name them.
A. Two
B. Three
C. Four
D. Five

18. ICO stands for?
A. Initial coin offering
B. Internal coin offering
C. Initial coin order
D. None of the above

19. How many kinds of ethereum applications are there? Name them.
    A. Two
    B. Three
    C. Four
    D. Five

20. Which one of these is designed to find the rates between two digital assets, making it trade crypto?
    A. Stellar's SDEX Exchange
    B. NEO'S NEX Exchange
    C. EtherDelta
    D. None of the above

Chapter 2: Blockchain Intermediate

Public Blockchain

A *Public Blockchain* is a block chaining network that is entirely open or public, and anyone having an account on that public blockchain and a transaction ID can join to participate. The network characteristically has an incentivizing mechanism to inspire more members to join. It is very important that the computational power is distributed globally without any primary focus in any specific geographical location.

All the public blockchain requires complex rules for increasing the security. It is the openness of public blockchain that implies little to no privacy for transactions and only supports a weak notion of security. The reason for the lack of security is that it is open to everyone. Hackers can always come and flood the blockchain for any bogus information or fraudulent transaction in the intentions to turn it down.

However, since they have the more complex rules to understand the flooding or the DDoS attacks, the public blockchain can protect itself automatically. Since the blockchain is public, there is no central authority, or there is no trusted third party. It always requires the complex consensus and hard times to make sure that the entire goal is to agree on a sustained transaction with the same decisions.

To accomplish consensus precisely, each node in a network needs to resolve a complex, resource-intensive cryptographic problem known as the proof of work to ensure all are synced.

There is no need of central authority or any trusted third-party. blockchain requires the complex consensus algorithm to make sure all entities agree upon a certain decision. Consensus algorithm is a decision-making process by the certain authorities (miners) who agree upon a decision. Consensus algorithm validates, authenticates and keeps the track of the transactions of a block. No single owner can claim the ownership or authenticity of the transaction; each transaction is resolved by miners. This evaluation of each transaction (proof of work) is further verified by miners with consensus.

Example:

In order to understand how public block chains works in real world, visit the following website

https://www.blockchain.com/explorer

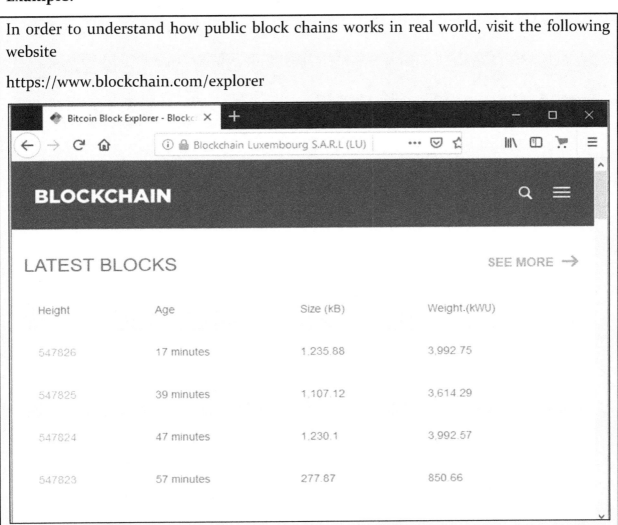

Now click on any Height value (Block)

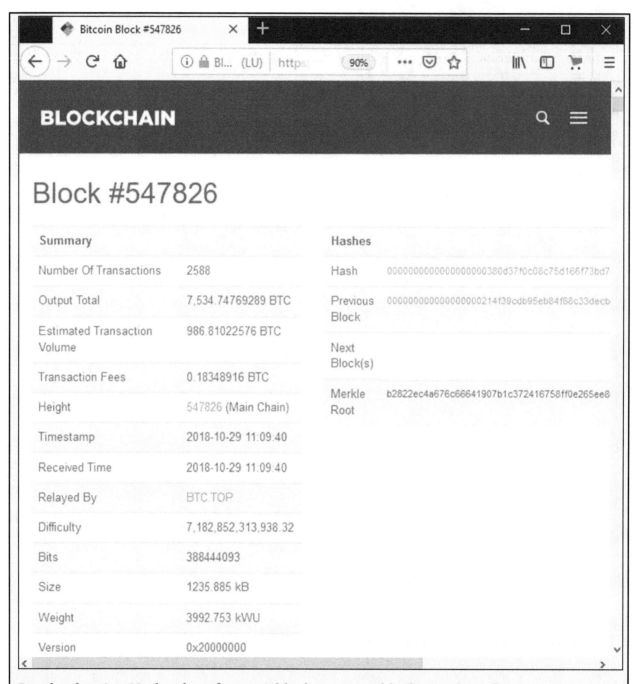

Results showing Hash value of current block, previous block, number of transactions, time stamp value, and much more.

Private Blockchain

Apart from public blockchains, there are private blockchains as well. These private blockchains require explicit permission or authorization to be accessed. It is similar to public blockchain but with access controls that restrict those who can join the chain. It means, private blockchains require an authorized node as an arbitrator that resolves the dispute among nodes. This arbitrator might be a centralized database that limits access to specific users. Applications include auditing, database management, and so forth. It might be a trusted third-party controlling the entire chain. It has one or multiple entities that control the network, leading to the reliance on third parties to transact.

Hence there can be a governing authority and a trusted third party who is maintaining and making sure that blockchain is safe, however the consensus can be resolved using the arbitrator. We can choose who becomes the arbitrator when there is no consensus.

A good way of taking advantage of blockchain technology is by setting up groups and participants who can verify transactions internally. It sets you at the risk of security breaches just similar to an integrated system, as opposed to public blockchain protected by game theoretic incentive mechanisms.

With the private blockchain, you need explicit authorization from the nodes. You can write or read the information as it is transitioning into the blockchain or from the blockchain. It is a private blockchain where security can implement in a very easy way by making someone responsible for it.

Furthermore, private blockchain is valuable for solving efficiency, security and fraud problems within traditional financial institutions, but only incrementally. It is not very likely that private blockchain revolutionizes the financial system.

Example:

RecordsKeeper is an example that offers both public and private block chaining. RecordsKeeper offers a full suite of structured and easily accessible record keeping technology for organizations and individuals. RecordsKeeper creates a platform for structured queryable storage of key-valued pair over the decentralized peer-to-peer network for ease of data access and security between peers. RecordsKeeper capitalizes on the benefits of blockchain technology to create an ecosystem for the secure transfer, authorization, integrity, and authenticity of data. Each peer is an autonomous agent, capable of performing these actions without significant human interactions.

For more information about Recordskeeper, please visit: www.recordskeeper.co

The Linux Foundation's Hyperledger Fabric is an example of a private blockchain structure execution and one of the Hyperledger projects hosted by The Linux Foundation. It was designed to ground up and accommodate to the enterprises' requirements.

P2P network

The blockchain is a direct node interaction, decentralized, computer network, also known as the peer-to-peer network. It represents a system or a network of interconnected computers that does not rely on a central party to facilitate interaction.

The blockchain is a decentralized distributed ledger that maintains a continuously growing number of transactions and data records. Transactions occur directly, without any intermediaries and central authority. These systems depend on consensus among many peers in the network to make changes to the chain.

Peer-to-Peer (P2P) represents the computers that participate in the network that are peers to each other, there are no single nodes, they are all equivalent, andt the nodes share the burden entirely of delivering network services.The network nodes connected in a mesh network with a flat topology. There is no hierarchy, no centralized service and no server inside the network.

Nodes in a peer-to-peer network both consume and deliver services at the same time with reciprocity performing as the incentive for participation. Peer-to-peer networks are open, decentralized and inherently robust. The famous example of P2P network architecture is the early Internet itself when nodes on the IP network had an equivalent value.

Blockchain's practical life example clears all the points that make sure that the blockchain is a P2P network.

Bitcoin is structured as a peer-to-peer network architecture that looks like an internet application such as Facebook and Twitter. It is a peer-to-peer digital cash system by design, and the network architecture is in cooperation with a reflection and a foundation of that essential representative. Decentralization is a core design principle, and can only be achieved and maintained by a flat, decentralized P2P consensus network.

Blockchain and Peer-to-Peer networks work in a similar domain that's why blockchain is also called a P2P network.They do not depend on a single server and centralized ledger.They work in decentralized server or ledger by means that connectthe nodes very

closely to related points or to other nodes. Moreover, they are defined in the upper part of the P2P network section.

Blocks

Block is an individual unit of blockchain containing records of some or all bitcoin transactions. These records are secured using Hashing algorithm to ensure the integrity of the information. It records a small number of or all the newest Bitcoin transactions that have not yet come into the prior blocks. Therefore, a block is similar to a record book or page of a ledger. For each an every time a block is completed, it provides a way to the next block in the blockchain. A block is consequently a permanent store of records, which once written, cannot be changed or deleted.

Transactions

Transaction in a blockchain system is defined as "Small unit of task recorded in a block". Transaction in blockchain is similar to banking transaction. Here the term transaction refers the transfer of bitcoins by one account holder to another. Since the transactions are not encrypted, any one in the blockchain can view and verify the transaction.

For Example

Let's visit https://www.blockchain.com/explorer again, and check the transaction.

Click on any block to view details

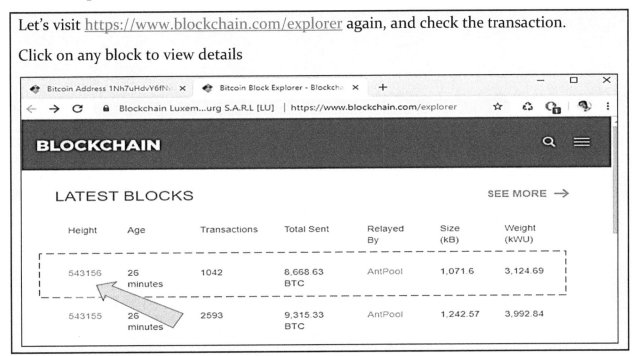

Now Click on any transaction of this block:

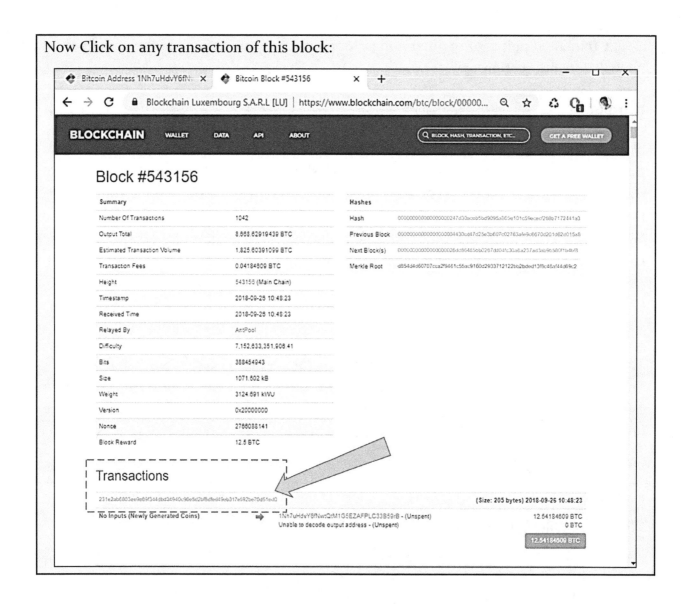

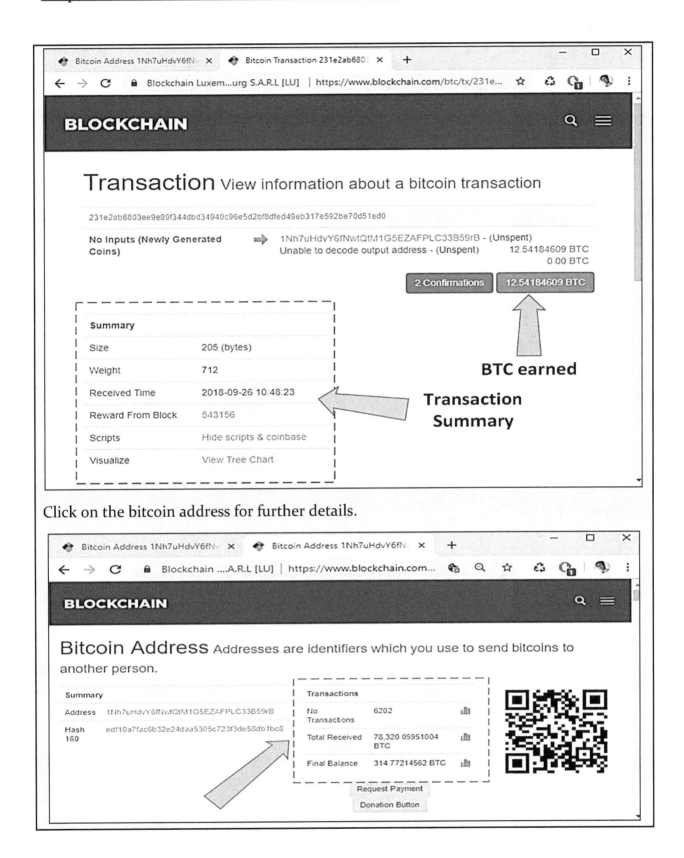

Click on the bitcoin address for further details.

Private Key

It is a secret key that allows bitcoins to be spent. Each bitcoin wallet holds one or more private keys in the wallet file. The private keys are mathematically related to all bitcoin addresses generated for the wallet. It is a key that is kept in secret to ensure it is not misused and is used for authentication and encryption. It securely sends information over an unencrypted network.

Here, the concept of Public Key Cryptography is used in blockchain technology. Public Key Cryptography relies on two keys; namely, **Public Key** and **Private Key**. These keys are calculated for the sake of secured communication. Public key is broadcasted all over the network so that anyone can encrypt the data using public key and send it to the recipient. Private key is kept secret so that encrypted messages can only be decrypted by the recipient itself. Apart from decrypting, private keys are also used to generate digital signatures to ensure the actual source of information or transaction. Bitcoin uses *Elliptic Curve Digital Signature Algorithm* (ECDSA). ECDSA generates private keys in such a secured and advanced way that it is impossible to get the corresponding private key of a public key.

This is used to create digital signatures, a piece of code that helps guarantee that the author of a transaction isthe individual who holds the private key. The digital signature along with the consistent public key helps to specify the identity of the user who sent the transaction.

Addresses

Address is the identifier to whom you are sending the bitcoins. Initially, bitcoin directly pays to the IP addresses using Pay-to-IP method. This method is now evolved into a more suitable method for the bitcoin transactions using Pay-to-Public-Key-Hash (P2PKH). A standard P2PKH address contains 34 alphanumeric symbols, beginning with a "1". Below is the example of a bitcoin address:

```
1K9g5MxFFTHchXpRhjHPi2zEXb31KZXjc0
```

Sample Transaction

A bitcoin transaction is an agreement of data that is shown to the network and, if legal, completed up in a block in the blockchain.

The objective of a bitcoin transaction is to transfer ownership of a certain amount of bitcoin to a bitcoin address.

When someone sends bitcoin, a single data structure, namely a bitcoin transaction, produces in your wallet client and then broadcasts it to the network. Bitcoin nodes on the network depend on the transaction and rebroadcast it. If the transaction is valid, nodes comprise it in the block that they are mining. Generally, within 10-20mins, the transaction has involved with other transactions in a block in the blockchain. At this instant, the receiver can see the transaction amount in their wallet.

Example

To better understand the transaction process in blockchain, consider Alice buying a cup of coffee from Bob's Café.

Alice is a new user who has just acquired her first bitcoin. When a new user joins the blockchain network, it requires a bitcoin. There are four methods to acquire bitcoin being a new user.

1. Find a friend and buy something from him.
2. Use classified service.
3. Sell a product or service for bitcoin.
4. Use your bitcoin ATM.

"To join the bitcoin network and start transactions, users have to download an application or login to a bitcoin web application. There are several implementations of the bitcoin client software. One of the reference implementation of bitcoin client software is known as the Satoshi client, which is managed as an open source project by a team of developers and is derived from the original implementation written by Satoshi Nakamoto. "

Alice met her friend Joe to exchange cash for bitcoin. The transaction generated by Joe funded Alice's wallet with 0.10 BTC. Now Alice can make her first retail transaction, purchasing a cup of coffee in Bob's coffee shop. Bob's coffee shop offers bitcoin transactions service on his Point-of-Sale sytem.

Bob has listed pricing in both US dollars as well as in BTC. Point-of-Sale system converts the amount in US Dollars into BTC if any customer wants to pay in BTC. Following is a sample bill of Alice at Bob's coffee shop.

Total:			
Item		Amount	
Cup of Coffee	x1	USD 1.50	0.015 BTC

In the next section, we will see how the transaction can occur and what is a bitcoin transaction.

Bitcoin Transactions

A transaction shows the network that the owner of bitcoins has authorized the transfer of some of those bitcoins to another owner. Now, the new owner can spend these bitcoins by creating another transaction that authorizes the transfer to another owner, and that is all there is in a chain of ownership.

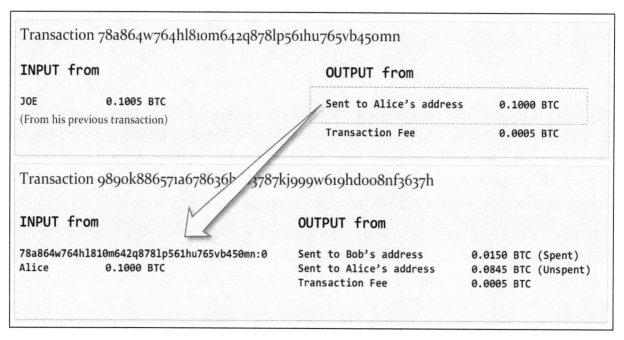

Figure 2-01: Sample Bitcoin Transaction

FigureA: Chain of transactions is where the output of a single transaction is the input of the next transaction.

Alice's payment to Bob's Cafe uses the last transaction as its input. In the previous chapter, Alice got some bitcoin from her friend Joe in return for cash. That transaction had some bitcoins locked (encumbered) against Alice's key. Her new transaction to Bob's Cafe

mentions the last transaction as an input and makes new outputs to pay on behalf of the cup of coffee and collects change. The transactions produce a chain, where the inputs from the latest transaction correspond to outputs from last transactions. Alice's key delivers the signature that unlocks those last transactions outputs, thus proving to the bitcoin network that she owns the funds. She assigns the payment for the coffee to Bob's address, thus "encumbering" that output with the requirement that Bob can produce a signature to spend that amount. It signifies a transfer of value between Bob and Alice. This chain of transactions, as of Joe to Alice to Bob, is demonstrated in Figure A.

Consensus

The consensus is a process of agreement between distrusting nodes on a final state of data. To achieve consensus, different algorithms can be used. It is easy to reach an agreement between two nodes (such as client-server systems), but when various nodes are participating in a distributed system and they need to agree on a single value, it becomes complicated to achieve consensus.

Consensus Mechanisms

It is a set of phases that are taken by all nodes to agree on a proposed state or value. It has recently come into the limelight and gained much popularity with the advent of bitcoin and blockchain.

There are various requirements that must be met to provide the desired results in a consensus mechanism. The followings are their requirements with brief descriptions:

Agreement: The whole honest nodes decide on the same value.

Fault tolerant: The consensus algorithm should be able to run in the presence of faulty or malicious nodes (Byzantine nodes).

Integrity: This is a requirement where no node can make the decision more than once. The nodes make decisions only once in a single consensus cycle.

Termination: The whole honest nodes terminate execution of the consensus process and eventually reach a decision.

Validity: The value agreed upon by all honest nodes must be the same as the initial value proposed by at least one honest node.

Types Of Consensus Mechanism

There are various types of consensus mechanism; some common types are shown here.

- Byzantine fault tolerance-based
- Leader-based consensus mechanisms

To explain how the consensus works and how the conflicts have resolved in the blockchain, let us take an example of a conflict.

Conflict Example:

Consider a blockchain with several nodes. All of the nodes are synchronized, the blockchain is at block number 200, and hence the new block will be the block number 201. As shown in the figure 2-02:

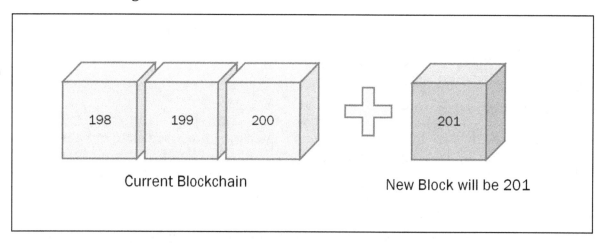

Figure 2-02: Adding new block into existing blockchain

As we know, there are several miners in a blockchain. For example, three miners have mined the new Block 201 at nearly the same time. Each newly created block will have a different signature, hence they will never be the same. Let us say that these newly created blocks are named as 201a, 201b and 201c.

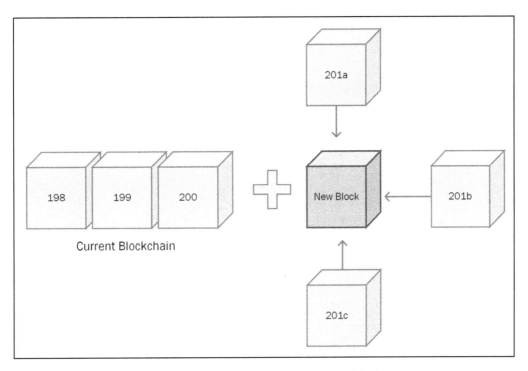

Figure 2-03: Conflict in adding new block

Here, the conflict that arises is which block will be finally added in the blockchain. Increasing the value of BTC and reward makes it a costly problem for the miners. These conflicts are generally resolved by using a method called the longest chain rule.

Longest Chain Rule

In a public blockchain like bitcoin, the conflicts can be easily handled with this rule. Let us say the miner received the block201 from different sources, it will start building the next block in branches. For example, in our case, if 201a, 201b and 201c are the blocks updated simultaneously. Upcoming blocks will be mined on top of their parent block. As a result, they become three branches; 201a, 201b and 201c.

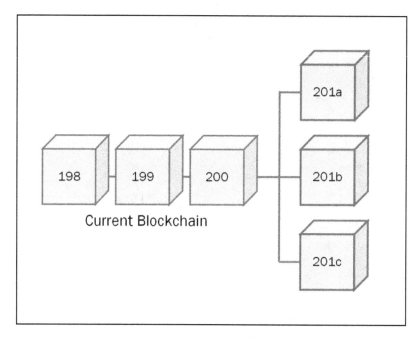

Figure 2-04: Longest chain rule

Now, back to our example, you can see that 201a, 201b, and 201c are the three new blocks mined at the same time. If a miner receives 202a first, it will start building the next block (202a) on top of its parent block (201a). When the miner sees another block e.g 202b and then 202c, the miner keeps an eye on these new block as well and consider them as branches.

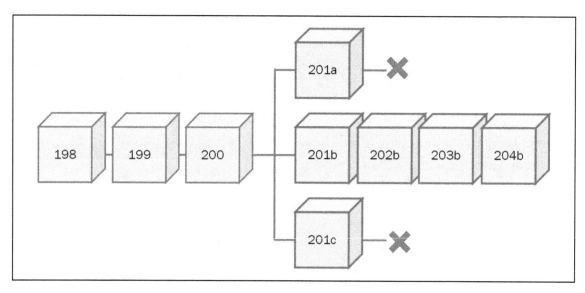

Figure 2-05: Longest chain rule

In our case, the new block 202b is detected by someone. If a certain miner tries to build on top of 201b and succeeds, then the 202b block will be announced in the network. Similarly, upcoming blocks will be added on the top of their parent blocks. Now 201b has the longest chain, miners will continue building on top of this block.

As a result, those miners who received 201a from the beginning, can now switch to the longest branch(201b) and we can discard the other branches (201a and 201c). This is called the longest blockchain rule because the blocks are interested in focusing on whoever has the longest blockchain and is considered trustworthy and safe. For this reason, it is called the longest chain rule.

Blockchain mining

It becomes very important to authenticate the miner, ensure that whoever is adding the new block into the blockchain is a legitimate miner and has contributed before. The purpose of this authentication is to add the true block into the blockchain and avoid false blocks. Therefore, proof of work is where the miners have to solve the puzzle.

In Proof-of-Stake, reputation of a particular miner is given, and relying on this reputation, the block is added.

Types of mining

There are two types of mining.

1. Solo Mining
2. Pool Mining

Solo Mining

Solo Mining is an individual mining process in which each miner computes the pending transactions alone. No one is contributing in this computation, it does not mean that every miner will be rewarded. Only the successful miner will get the reward and others will get nothing. To perform solo mining, a machine that is capable of computing the hashes is required.

According to the blockchain council, the best way of getting your own blocks is "If you do the process of solo mining, make sure to connect your miner to your local bitcoin client"

It will be helpful to find your own block.

Pool Mining

A blockchain with pool mining is based on a contributed mining process. Each miner contributes its part of computation and gets partial share based on its contribution. Usually, we can search for a group of miners operating as a one sharing their processing power through a network, to divide the reward equally; according to the amount of work, they take partin the probability of searching a block and helping hands to decrease the return on the volatility.

Proof of Work v/s Proof of stake v/s Delegated POS v/s Proof of Importance

Proof of Work, Proof of Stake, Delegated POS, Proof of Importance; all of them have one mechanism in common. They are all block chaining algorithms that are applied on transactions to validate & verify the authenticity of a block & its transactions. It becomes significant when we start to think of mechanisms such as double spending. It is when the money is being spent more than once (illegally). For example, few currencies use verification of every transaction in the blockchain to avoid this situation.

Let us take a moment to explain a Proof-of-Work, then continue to the Proof-of-Stake and then continue to the delegated POS and Proof-of-Importance.

Proof of Work

- It is the unique consensus algorithm in a blockchain.
- The core operational mechanism is a complex mathematical puzzle to prove the solution quickly.
- Miners take part in the blockchain network against each other to complete transactions and get rewarded.
- The algorithm is used to verify the legitimacy of each transaction in order to avoid double-spending.
- Create new digital currencies for miners to reward.
- A decentralized ledger collects all the transactions into blocks.
- The most well-known applications are Bitcoin and Ethereum.

Proof of stake

- It is also a mechanism for confirming the transactions, hence the objective is the same as the proof of work, however, the results are achieved through different methods.
- New block is created in deterministic way depending upon wealth or stake.
- No block reward in Proof of Stake, hence miners only get the transaction fee.
- Proof of Stake eliminates the heavy computational power requirements.
- It is more rapid and efficient than the Proof of work system, as technically everyone might become a miner.
- It proposes a linear scale related to the numbers of blocks that a miner may authorize since it is based on the cryptocurrency.

Proof of Work	Proof of Stake
It is a significant and expensive computer calculation called mining blocks.	The miner of a new block in the blockchain is selected in a deterministic method depending on wealth (stake).
A reward is given to the initial miner who resolves each block calculation.	The miners do not receive a block reward but collect network fees as the reward.
Miners complete using computer power initially to search a solution.	This mechanism creates Proof of Stake mining which is much more energy efficient.

Table 2-01: Proof-of-Work vs Proof-of-Stake

Delegated Proof of Stake (DPOS)

It has a newer consensus model that was invented by Dan Larimer as a consensus framework for Bitshares and is applied to various platforms such as Lisk (LSK), Steem, and EOS. It is, to some extent, similar to PoS but has diverse and more "democratic" features that makes it more efficient and fair.

It is the most efficient, fastest, most decentralized, and most flexible consensus model available. It uses a reputation system and real-time voting to achieve consensus. Community members vote for super representatives to secure their network. The super representatives are rewarded by validating transactions for the next block.

It's objectives are to produce better incentives and a fast, accessible, more distributed and more efficient consensus mechanism.

It influences the power of stakeholder approval, voting to resolve consensus issues in a fair and democratic way. All network parameters, from fee schedules to block intervals and transaction sizes, can tune via elected delegates. Deterministic selection of block producers allows transactions to confirm in an average of just 1 second. Most importantly, the consensus protocol was designed to protect all participants against unwanted regulatory interference.

It mostly represents a liquid, which means representative is a type of democracy consensus format that makes essential tweaks from the typical Proof of Stake model and noticeable concessions when it comes to decentralization.

It is more decentralized than other consensus systems since the threshold to enter is very low. Another alternative is to generally "allow" anyone to enter, but most people are excluded from entering due to high costs or needs, and generally, a few pools or large number of miners produce blocks on those systems.

Delegates get rewards on behalf of validating transactions, same as PoS, so cheating again makes littleto no sense as they lose both their role and their stake in the system. The rewards they do get,they can spend on lobbying, spreading the word about the currency, or cashing it out into earnings.

Few DPoS systems process in such ways that they can describe a burn rate; a percentage of tokens is given to destroy upon getting a reward.

It is the same as with PoS; its environment is very friendly and easy to execute on smaller and weaker devices. It is hard to stop because it does not depend on external factors controlled by the state, like electricity.

Differences between Proof of Stake and DPoS

Governance

Proof of Stake systems has the parameters programmed and blockchain's rules on the genesis block. Subsequently, any changes mean a fork in the protocol.

An elected panel of delegates by DPoS systems can propose changes to the protocol and actively govern the blockchain changes to the protocol, although for them to come into effect, the users must approve the changes.

Block creation

- In Proof of Stake systems, the designer of a new block is chosen in a pseudo-random way, depending on the user's coins at stake.
- In DPoS systems, users vote to elect some witnesses. The top tier of witnesses (typically 20) is rewarded for creating blocks and verifying transactions.
- DPoS is more rapid due to a significantly smaller number of users creating blocks and verifying transactions; DPoS is, therefore, more accessible.
- The main difference between DPoS and PoS is that in the DPoS's consensus system, community members have more governance rights in the network.

To better understand the DPoS, let us use a real-life scenario.

"It is as same as our democracy system; we can vote for people who will "mine" for the coins. People with more coins have more votes, hence, instead of everyone being able to "invest", we can now choose which people can invest."

For Example:

A burn rate of 40% destroys 40% of the tokens received by a delegate. ***"Burn rate is the rate at which a company is losing money".*** Destroying tokens leads to deflation, which leads to an increased value of the remaining tokens. Both of those tokens are in the hands of the delegates, however the tokens are also in people's wallets around the world. It is as everyone who uses the currency gets dividends because their money becomes more valuable. The remaining 60% of the tokens still is used as the delegate wants them.

Proof-of-Importance (POI)

It is the blockchain consensus algorithm that was first introduced by NEM. A mechanism that was used to determine which network participants mean that nodes are eligible to add a block to the blockchain.

It can be regarded as a novel consensus algorithm because of different existing consensus mechanisms.

For example:

Proof of Stake(POS): It seeks to take into account of one's overall support of the network.

POI systems do not only get rewarded with a large account balance but also takes into account of how much they transact to others and whom they transact it with.

Also, this rewarding is done through harvesting, a process in which a node calculates blocks, and adds it to the blockchain.

Harvesting is the term for mining blocks. It helps the network confirm the transaction and stay secured. As a reward, you collect your network fees based on your importance in the whole network. Your importance in the network is the trust scored. It is calculated based on how much you use the network. It means that those who actively use NEM gradually increase in importance.

POI ensures that people who use NEW can benefit the most. Moreover, it keeps the network secured and is environmentally friendly.

NEM

Many of the top blockchains, such as Litecoin and Bitcoin Cash, are also hard forks or software branches of the original Bitcoin code and blockchain. Nevertheless, this is not the case with NEM. It is built with a 100% original code. It has done away with Proof-of-Work and Proof-of-Stake as a replacement. NEM is the first cryptocurrency to use the "Proof-of-Importance" algorithm.

Security

It is innately secured and utilizes powerful cryptography to give individuals ownership of an address and the crypto assets (another way of referring to a cryptocurrency) associated with it, through a combination of public and private keys. It solves the issue of stolen identity, as addresses are not directly associated with users' identity, while also being far inflexible to co-operate. Even more, private keys are secured as they are significantly longer. It is the only way that blockchain can offer a higher level of security to the specific user as it eliminates the need for weak and certainly compromised passwords and online identities.

It stores data using sophisticated math and innovative software rules that are extremely difficult for attackers to manipulate.

There are many reasons for blockchain to improve data security; some are described below:

The blockchain can be private or public

We know about the inherent security risks in blockchain technology, it is vital to know the difference between public and private blockchain.

- Bitcoin applications are on a public blockchain, it is a system that records transactions and suggests to read or write transactions. Everyone can aggregate and

carry out those transactions; provided they can determine that a sufficient quantity of effort went into doing the process, which they can display by solving a tricky cryptographic puzzle.

- Designers who design to work on public blockchain systems like bitcoin still focuses on specific users to assume some alteration that they proposed, which helps to make sure that changes are only accepted if they are in the notice of the whole system. In a private blockchain, the operator is on the contrary and may decide to deploy changes with which some users may disagree individually.

- It is widely used in the financial area; private blockchain offers their operators to control more than who can read the ledger of the confirmed transactions, who can present transactions, and who can confirm them. The applications for private blockchain contain a range of markets in which many parties wish to contribute simultaneously. However, they do not entirely trust one another.

- When the problems of structure of financial market or other infrastructure on a public blockchain give the first applicant a pause, the private blockchain provides a degree of control over both participants' behavior and deals with the verification procedures.

- Private Blockchain operators can accomplish who has the right to work a node, and also, how those nodes are linked; a node with more links get information faster.

Blockchain is decentralized

Decentralization sometimes may run into unexpected consequences; Since everyone can read and write transactions, bitcoin transactions are being operated in a black market trading. The consensus protocol is energy consuming, number of users operate in countries with low-cost electricity, leading to a network centralization and the possibility of collusion, making the network vulnerable to changes in policy on electricity subsidies. Both of these trends have ran to an increased interest in the private blockchain that might eventually provide businesses a more considerable degree of control.

Private Blockchain owners have to make decisions about whether, and under what circumstances, to inverse a valid transaction, mostly if that transaction shows to be a theft. Transaction reverse can undermine confidence in the equality and fairness of the system; However, the system allows extensive losses because of the misuse of bug lose users. It is illustrated as a DAO (Decentralized Autonomous Organization) in latest case, a code-based scheme capital fund designed to run on Ethereum, a public blockchain-based platform. Security weaknesses in the code are operating the DAO to run the financial damages that require Ethereum developers to make some changes to the Ethereum protocol itself, even

though the DAO's vulnerabilities were not the fault of the Ethereum protocol. This is the conclusion that makes these changes controversial and highlights the indication that both public and private blockchain designers must consider the circumstances in which they would make the same decisions.

The blockchain is virtually impossible to hack

The blockchain cannot be hacked. The security of blockchain technologycannot behacked because it is carried out on cryptocurrency exchanges. Ordinary hack is the vulnerability that allows hackers to transfer stems from centralization. Even though blockchain technology has decentralized, there are still centralized aspects of it, such as cryptocurrency exchanges. It means that the hackers can attack a single point in the hope of gaining access. For example, those type of attacks gives rise to calls for decentralized exchanges, and it is a matter of time before these come to the main platform allowing people to trade cryptocurrencies.

Such hacks epitomize how crucial it is for each aspect of the blockchain to be as decentralized as possible, as distributed information and assets are more secured.

Financial information is a cross of network of computers, the mission of co-operating data comes to be much more difficult for hackers. Instead of consuming to breach only a single server, creating a fraudulent transaction or altering the balance on a blockchain can only be accomplished if the number of the network was compromised. A single server hacking can be very challenging, even for the most accomplished cybercriminals. Being able to compromise sufficient servers to fake records on the blockchain is virtually incredible, especially as hackers would need to breach every node simultaneously.

It is the highest level of security afforded by the distributed ledger system, making it particularly attractive to financial institutions, however, bitcoin offers some benefits to banks. Nevertheless, the same technology that supports the blockchain can be used to establish secured networks for any form of application, not only bitcoin.

Blockchain offers encryption and validation

- Encryption and blockchain transactions are the privacy-enhancing technologies that can be seen throughout network nodes. These produce statistical analysis and metadata can reveal information even from encrypted data, allowing pattern recognition.

- Users rely on the privacy of the blockchain. If Keys are held securely and are encrypted, there will not be any issue. In many ways, a centralized system is less secured than the blockchain system.
- The blockchain is a decentralized ledger that can reduce costs by removing intermediaries such as decentralizing trust and bank. The technology appends entries to the ledger that are validated by the wider user-community rather than by a central authority.
- The system that ensures the validators have permission to the system making its owners feel more secured. However, it only gives them more control, which means they can make changes whether or not other network participants agree. This means that the right believers will be seen as violating the right ideas of the blockchain.

Let us see an example to understand what makes blockchains "secure" in principle.

For Example:

Bitcoin is a good example

The shared data is the history of all Bitcoin transaction ever made; an accounting ledger. The ledger is stored in numerous copies on a network of the processor, called "nodes." For each time someone submits a transaction to the ledger, the nodes check to guarantee the transaction is legal meaning that whoever spends a bitcoin has a bitcoin to spend. A subset of these competes to pack valid transactions into "blocks" and adds them to a chain of previous ones. The owner of these nodes are known as miners. It is the person who successfully adds new blocks to the chain and earns bitcoins as a reward.

This makes the system theoretically tamperproof with its two effects;

- A cryptographic fingerprint is unique for each block.
- A consensus protocol is processed by the nodes in the network that agree on a shared history.

Secured Blockchain Usage Worldwide:

Countries and multinational firms use blockchain because of its security and effectiveness.

- Two major Australian banks have successfully used blockchain for bank guarantees relating to commercial property, leasing of a shopping center operator. The digitized

- guarantee created a single information source with lower fraud potential and greater efficiency.
- Block chain's "irreversible" and encrypted data blocks can also help fight cybercrime, as a hacker's attempts to change data will be flagged immediately. As applications of blockchain for cybersecurity emerge, companies and governments are signing up.
- US defense contractor Lockheed Martin announced last year that they are integrating blockchain into systems, engineering supplychain that risk management and software development.
- Several Indian states are exploring blockchain-based systems to improve information efficiency and enhance cybersecurity. In 2017, Andhra Pradesh signed up with the Swiss cybersecurity company WISeKey International to ensure citizens' information stored in databases remains secured with blockchain.

Attacks

There are many techniques used to hack a blockchain. These techniques depend upon the vulnerability & loopholes in the blockchaining system. Before explaining these techniques, some of the real attacks are described here.

"In August, a team of hackers called, "51 Crew" attacked blockchain Krypton and clones shift. The team took the access of more than 51% of the network. After that, there was the online theft of $65 million of the digital currency bitcoin fromBitfinx; It is an Hong Kong-based exchange. The most dangerous hacking event was in May 2016, when a hacker abusing a weakness in its smooth contract code, allocating a blow of around $60 million, attacked the Decentralized Autonomous Organization (DAO). It ran into a dividing of the Ethereum blockchain, into Ethereum and Ethereum Classic."

It is a DNS attack that runs to co-operate passwords for bitcoin end users.

Software Vulnerabilities

In any software or application, the most significant attack vector is human error. The significant losses of funds seen so far in cryptoland are the result of bugs in the software of the coin itself. Cryptographic errors in the security of cryptocurrencies leave security holes that can be discovered and exploited by sophisticated hackers to undermine a project.

The DAO example showed us that the software is developed by humans and may sometimes subject to human error. When most of the blockchain applications done for bitcoin have been verified over the years, many weaknesses were recognized, we cannot

guarantee that there is no more. Additionally, number of companies like the Ethereum platform, use it as a structure and later modify it. They provide flexibility to designers to write their smart contracts, therefore opening more ways for conceivable bugs.

To ease this, the Software Development Lifecycle (SDLC) and Quality Assurance (QA) testing process want to have enormously more robust. When much attention is paid to necessary or functional testing, white-box and black box security testing need more emphasis.

We anticipate that initially numerous platforms deliver partial functionality (such as asset issuance), limiting the possibility for attacks due to the cause of programmer errors.

Private key Compromise

It is the most direct way to hack into a blockchain network. Each user has a private key with which they sign transactions, and anyone on the network can verify the transaction utilizing their public key to assess if the original user has signed it. If a private key was stolen, all the digital currency associated with it could be compromised. The thief can sign a transaction to transfer all the bitcoins to his address directly.

These wallets consume security features to protect an enduser's private key and can have access from multiple devices, including a cloud-based one. It also provides a range of services including distributing public keys, signing transactions, and broadcasting the transactions to peer-to-peer networks.

Proof of Work hacked into computing power

Proof of work networks are same as bitcoin, lots of computing powers are used to prove that a transaction is genuine. If more than 50% of the bitcoin network participants agree to block, it will be deemed as accepted. In this scenario, anyone who can hack into machines and divert the computing power to his account, can control huge pieces of the network. It would allow the hacker to create a chain longer than the authentic chain, essentially allowing a dual transaction.

It mitigates this; various platforms are moving towards "proof of stake" consensus. It ensures that instead of computing power, the ability to approve a transaction is dependent on the stake of the participants that are in the network. People who have invested in a currency do not want its value crashing by ratifying rogue transactions.

For permissioned blockchains, the addition of nodes is a controlled activity, it would be hard for a hacker to control over the network. Some multinational corporations'

applications are likely to use permissioned blockchains with some level of oversight from a governing body or participants themselves.

It is particularly rare for a specific person to have their identity compromised by being hacked. Instead, it is through some of the biggest hacks, among the world's largest companies, that hackers obtain the most personal information. Countless multinational companies harvest as much information about their users as possible to increase the effectiveness of their sales teams. This data is nowhere near as secure as it needs to be. Those large organizations often fail to secure their databases, putting millions of their customers at serious risk.

Practice Questions

1. Asymmetric encryption uses:
   A. Proof of Stake
   B. Public and Private keys
   C. Public keys only
   D. Private keys only

2. What is a private key?
   A. A key that opens a secret door
   B. A key on your keychain
   C. A key does not give access to the public
   D. A key gives access to the public

3. What incentivizes the miners to give true validation of transactions?
   A. More memory
   B. A nonce
   C. Thumbs up from the community
   D. A block reward

4. What is the purpose of a nonce?
   A. Send information to the Blockchain network
   B. A hash function
   C. Follow nouns

D. Prevent double spending

5. What is a DAPP?
   A. A Decentralized Application
   B. A type of Cryptocurrency
   C. A condiment
   D. A type of Blockchain

6. Which is NOT a form of asymmetric encryption?
   A. Mining
   B. Passphrase
   C. Private Key
   D. Public key

7. What are the different types of tokens?
   A. Platform
   B. Privacy
   C. Currency
   D. All of the above

8. Where is the LEAST SAFE place to retain your Cryptocurrency?
   A. In your pocket
   B. At your work desk
   C. On an exchange
   D. On a hot wallet

9. Who created Bitcoin?
   A. Samsung
   B. John Mcafee
   C. Satoshi Nakamoto
   D. China

10. What does P2P stand for?
    A. Product to Product

    B. Private Key to Public Key

    C. Password to Password

    D. Peer to Peer

11. What is a node?

    A. A Blockchain

    B. A computer on a Blockchain network

    C. A type of cryptocurrency

    D. An exchange

12. Where do you store your cryptocurrency?

    A. Wallet

    B. In your pocket

    C. Bank account

    D. Floppy Disk

13. What is a miner?

    A. A person who performs calculations to verify a transaction

    B. Computers that validate and process Blockchain transactions

    C. A form of a blockchain

    D. An algorithm that expects the next part of the chain

14. Where can you buy a cryptocurrency?

    A. A Bitcoin ATM

    B. A private transaction

    C. An exchange

    D. All of the above

15. What is a blockchain?

    A. An exchange

    B. A centralized ledger

    C. A peer to peer network on a distributed ledger

    D. A form of Cryptocurrency

16. Which is the term for when a Blockchain splits?
    A. A fork
    B. A division
    C. A merger
    D. A sidechain

17. What is cold storage?
    A. The Internet is connected to the private key
    B. The Internet is not connected to the private key
    C. A place to hang your coat
    D. A paper wallet

18. What is a genesis block?
    A. The first block after each block
    B. The 2nd transaction of a blockchain
    C. The first block of a blockchain
    D. A well-known block that is hardcoded with a hash of the Book of Genesis onto the blockchain

19. What powers the Ethereum Virtual Machine?
    A. Bitcoin
    B. Block Rewards
    C. Gas
    D. Ether

20. What is Proof of Stake?
    A. How private keys are made
    B. A transaction and block verification protocol
    C. A certificate needed to use the Blockchain
    D. A password needed to access an exchange

Chapter 3: Blockchain Advanced

Private Blockchain

As the name describes itself, private blockchains are the isolated blockchains that require an explicit authorization from the nodes that can actually read or write the information as a transaction into the blockchain or from the blockchain. In other words, private blockchain is accessible only to those who get the permissions from the authorized parties; it may be an individual or an organization. These blockchains are not publically available, but are only for the authorized members.

Following are the features of private blockchain:

- Only authorized nodes can read and write the ledger information
- Implementation of security becomes easy
- One authorized node can be the authority for any dispute
- Single or multiple private entities can own the blockchain
- Many legal authorities can be given to one party

Can I Setup my own Blockchain?

Yes, ofcourse, you can easily setup your own blockchain and become the owner of the blockchain that is controlled by you, and you are responsible for its security. Although, keeping a few things in mind, you have to take care of miners and setup your own miners.

There are many ways to setup your own Private Blockchain, some of them are described below.

Ethereum

Ethereum is one of the best example of the private blockchain. Private blockchain can be easily setup by private Ethereum blockchain by using Ethereum clients like Geth, C++ or python clients.

To setup private blockchain in Ethereum, these steps should be followed:

Custom Genesis File: Customize the Genesis file that contains the data including settings and configurations of the Genesis block.

Custom Data Directory: Customize the data directory that stores all the synchronize data according to the requirements.

Custom Network ID: Customize the network ID as a random number rather than 1 2 3 4 5 6 7 8 because they are using as reserved ID.

Disable Node Discovery: At last, disable the node discovery so no one can approach the private blockchain network unless they have the authority's permission.

Multichain

Multi-chain is one of the most simplifiedmethods to develop private blockchain. Multi-chain is an open source platform and is founded by Mr. Gideon Greenspan. It has many remarkable features like permissions, data streams, etc. By using these features, you can record the valuable data and retrieved them from the blockchain at any given time.

Hyperledger Fabric

Private blockchain can be setup by Hyperledger fabric because it does not have the concept of Mining or Cryptocurrency. Hyperledger Fabric is mainly contributed by IBM. Hyperledger is the project hosted by Linux foundation, *Umbrella* and *Fabric* are the projects hosted under the Hyperledger's project. Hence, private blockchain can be easily setup by using Hyperledger fabric at any time. IBM also offers private blockchain setup using IBM bluemix platform.

OpenChain

Openchain is one of the ways to setup private blockchain. Openchain is an open source distributed ledger mechanism.

Following are the fundamentals to setup the Openchain as a private blockchain:

- An individual can spin up a new Openchain instance in a few seconds.
- The administrator of an Openchain instance defines the rules of the ledger.
- End-users can interchange value on the ledger according to the rules defined by the administrator.
- Each transaction on the ledger is digitally signed.

When to use a Blockchain & when NOT?

When to Use a Blockchain

Blockchain is a powerful technology that is flourishing in many businesses and private areas.

The blockchain is best suited in the following scenarios:

Share Common Database: When organizations need to share a common database across their employees, contractors, or third parties, the permissioned blockchain can fit into this situation.

Conflict Incentives: When parties involved with the process have conflict incentives or they have trust issues among participants.

Transaction Policy: When business models require a simple or complex policy to perform any transaction, blockchain can be extremely helpful by using its logical policies such as Ethereum or Hyperledger.

System Transparency: When parties decide that the system must be transparent to their customers or suppliers. Hence, a permissionless blockchain network is used to fulfil the requirements.

Data Immutability: When businesses process data that has been passed through many different databases. To sustain the consistency of the data across all transactions, blockchain is needed.

When NOT to Use blockchain

Although Blockchain is a great technology for many areas, it may not suitable for some cases.

Some scenarios are described here:

Store Large Data: As you know, blockchain is distributive in nature, so it does not store large string of data. Therefore, blockchain is not useful in such cases.

Rules of Transactions: Organizations with frequently changing business process rules are not recommended to use blockchain-based applications.

Extract Data: Blockchain is not for using for the extraction of data taken place from outside the source.

How to build your own Blockchain Solution?

As discussed earlier, we can setup our own blockchain according to our convenience. The following section will describe the method to build your own blockchain solution.

It takes several major steps.

Step 01: Defining the Goal

Every business process initiates with defining the goal and purpose. Building your own blockchain might be a difficult task if you cannot identify the problem and have the ability to solve it. Blockchain has gotten extensive hype due to their misconceptions. Blockchain building starts with appropriate goal that it is beneficial for you.

Step 02: Specify the most favorable Consensus Method

After defining the goal, it is time to take some steps towards its completion. According to your use-case, you have to select the most reliable and advantageous consensus method.

As blockchain is a decentralized network, it requires all the members of the network to authenticate a transaction, this process is called consensus. For example, Bitcoin uses proof of work as a consensus mechanism.

Step 03: Specify the Most Suitable Platform

According to your selected consensus mechanism, you have to select the most suitable blockchain platform. Now a day, many platforms facilitate blockchain, most of them are free and open source.

Some popular blockchain platforms outline there:

- Ethereum
- Corda
- Chain Core
- Hyperledger Fabric
- Multichain
- Openchain

Step 04: Designing the Architecture

Another important step is designing the blockchain architecture. At this stage, decide whether the node will run on the cloud, on the premises or both, then decide which hardware and operating systems are suitable.

Step 5: Designing the Blockchain Instance

This is a very crucial step as blockchain instances are designed here.

Configure the blockchain instances below carefully:

1. Permissions
2. Asset issuance
3. Asset re-issuance
4. Atomic exchanges
5. Key management
6. Multi signatures
7. Parameters
8. Native assets
9. Address formats
10. Key formats
11. Block signatures
12. Hand-shaking

Step 6: Building the APIs

Many platforms have pre-built API while some do not. There are major considerations that you will have to address while building an API;

- Generating key pairs and addresses.
- Performing audit related functions.
- Data authentication through digital signatures and hashes.
- Data storage and retrieval.
- Smart-asset lifecycle management relating to issuance, payment, exchange, escrow and retirement.
- Smart contracts.

Step 7: Designing the Admin-User Interface

At this step, decision is required relating to the front-end programming language, servers and external database for the application.

Step 8: Integrate Upcoming Technology

Blockchain solution can be integrated by emerging technologies to enhance its capability.

Few integrating technologies are mentioned here:

- Artificial Intelligence
- Biometrics
- Cloud
- Cognitive services
- Internet of Things
- Machine Learning

Working with Blockchain Architecture

The blockchain is an emerging technology that has taken the world by storm. This part of the book explains the operation of blockchain architecture. This section will comprise of several norms such as Blocks, Nodes, Transaction, Ledger, Reward and Validation.

Generally, a blockchain technology comprises of numbers of nodes fashioned in a decentralized network holding a copy of a ledger. The decentralized ledger keeps record of all transactions that are performed over the peer-to-peer network. The major spark of this technology is that it facilitates the market individuals to transfer money across the internet without requesting the central authority.

A step- by- step architectural work of blockchain with a graphical view is represented here:

Step 01: Proposed Transaction

Blockchain processing begins with the person requesting for a transaction in the blockchain.

Step 02: P2P Network

The requested transaction is introduced to a Peer-to-Peer network that contains nodes. The transaction requires authorization of all the nodes for further processing.

Step 03: Validation & Verification

These nodes validate the transaction and the user's status by using appropriate algorithms. Verification of transaction can include cryptocurrency, contracts, records, or other information.

Step 04: Create a New Block

When the transaction has been verified by all the nodes of the network, the transaction is combined with the existing transactions to create a new block of data for the ledger.

Step 05: Add a New Block

The new block becomes a part of the existing blockchain with verified data, and now the data cannot be modified.

Step 06: Transaction Complete

The work of blockchain architecture completes the requested transaction that becomes a permanent part of the blockchain.

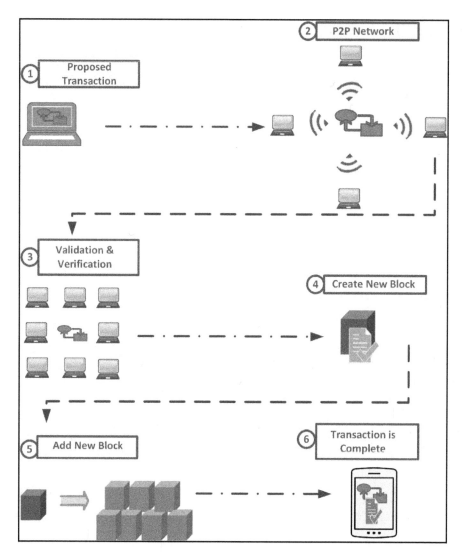

Figure 3-01: Blockchain Architecture

Smart Contracts

The smart contract is a terminology used to define software program code that has the facilitating, executing, and enforcing capability to negotiate the performance of a contract with Blockchain technology. It is an agreement between the two parties that have agreed upon the rules directing a business transaction.

The whole process is fully automated and can perform as complement or substitute for legal contracts. This places the conditions of the smart contracts that are coded in a programming language like C+/C++, Java, Python as a set of instructions.

In simplest meaning, smart contracts are programs that are written to perform specific execution by their developer. Even though contracts can be encoded on any blockchain platform, Ethereum is the most preferred choice because it provides scalable processing capabilities. Ethereum permits developers to code their own smart contracts.

Smart contracts can be used to:

- Update the process of claim clearings by automatically triggering a claim when specific events happen.
- Manage agreements between the users.
- Store information about application such as health records.

Smart Contract Works

The process of smart contract includes three main steps;

1. **Coding:** It is a pre-defined coding stored in a blockchain by a smart contract developer. Codes are defined according to users' interest in a difficult task; it behaves as the user want.

2. **Execution**: If the pre-defined rules are to settle down, then it distributes ledgers among all the nodes of a network. If any network meets the agreement, the event is triggered, and the transaction is executed as per the coded terms.

3. **Settlement:** When both parties agree upon the coded execution, the network updates the distributed ledgers to document the execution of the contract, and then monitors for compliance with the terms of the smart contract.

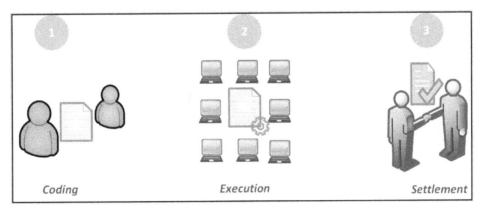

Figure 3-02: Smart Contract Works

Practice Questions

1. Which of the following is a permissioned blockchain?
   A. Public
   B. Private
   C. Consortium
   D. None of the above

2. Which of the following is a permissionless blockchain?
   A. Public
   B. Private
   C. Consortium
   D. None of the above

3. In private blockchain, authorize nodes can _____ the ledger information.
   A. Read
   B. Write
   C. Read & write
   D. All of the above

4. When you setup your own blockchain, what is the most important thing to own?
   A. Ledger
   B. Nonce
   C. Miners
   D. Hashes

5. Which of the following platform can be used to setup our own Blockchain?
   A. OpenChain
   B. Multichain
   C. Ethereum
   D. Hyperledger Fabric
   E. All of the above

6. Which blockchain platform is founded by Mr. Gideon Greenspan?
    A. OpenChain
    B. Multichain
    C. Ethereum
    D. Hyperledger Fabric

7. Which blockchain platform does not have the concept of mining & cryptocurrency?
    A. OpenChain
    B. Multichain
    C. Ethereum
    D. Hyperledger Fabric

8. Which project is hosted by Linux foundation umbrella?
    A. Hyperledger
    B. OpenChain
    C. Multichain
    D. Ethereum

9. Blockchain technology is not used in the following situation;
    A. Data Immutability
    B. Store Large Data
    C. Share Common Database
    D. System Transparency

10. Blockchain technology is the most suitable for?
    A. Frequently changing rules of transaction
    B. Extraction of data from outsource
    C. Share common database
    D. Store large data

11. Which step is the beginning to setup our own blockchain?
    A. Specify the most favorable Consensus Method

   B. Defining the Goal
   C. Designing the Architecture
   D. Integrate Upcoming Technology

12. Which one of them is an optional part but enhances the features of your blockchain?
   A. Building APIs
   B. Defining the Goal
   C. Admin- user Interface
   D. Integrating Upcoming Technology

13. Which is not the consideration of Building APIs?
   A. Generating key pairs and addresses
   B. Performing audit related functions
   C. Designing the Admin-User Interface
   D. Storing and retrieving data

14. Each blockchain contains which of the following?
   A. A hash pointer to the previous block
   B. Timestamp
   C. List of transactions
   D. All of the above

15. How many parent nodes are present in a Decentralized network?
   A. One
   B. More than one
   C. No parent node
   D. Only child node

16. In a P2P network, all nodes are designed in such a way that
   A. All nodes are connected to each other
   B. Each node can communicate with each other
   C. If one node fails, the other will work

D. All of the above

17. The working of blockchain begins with
    A. Creating a new block
    B. Adding a new block
    C. Anyone requesting for transaction
    D. Verification & validation of new block

18. In which of the following step, consensus mechanism is applied?
    A. Creating a new block
    B. Adding a new block
    C. Validation & Verification
    D. Requesting for transaction

19. After validation & verification of transaction which process occurs?
    A. Creating a new block
    B. Adding a new block
    C. Transaction is completed
    D. Requested for transaction

20. Created block with verified data cannot be _____.
    A. Stored
    B. Modified
    C. Read
    D. Written

21. The architectural working of Blockchain ends with?
    A. Creating a new block
    B. Adding a new block
    C. Transaction is completed
    D. Requested for transaction

22. Smart contract works on the principle of
    A. Smart developer
    B. Smart user
    C. Smart coding
    D. Smart transaction

23. Which platform is the most suitable for Smart contract?
    A. Hyperledger
    B. OpenChain
    C. Multichain
    D. Ethereum

24. In working with smart contract, triggering an event occurs by?
    A. Nodes
    B. Coding
    C. Distributed ledger
    D. Transaction

25. In a blockchain, each blockchain is linked with _____.
    A. Previous Block
    B. Next Block
    C. Not linked
    D. None of the above

Chapter 4: Blockchain Use-cases

Supply-chain

We know that blockchain is an emerging technology popularly known for its cryptocurrency application, i.e. bitcoin. The blockchain is a distributed ledger tracking digital assets on the P2P network. Its' applications are not limited to a particular nature of business, it can be implemented for the documents of agreements/contracts, payments, transactions, and any exchange of resources. Major advantage of implementing blockchain is the transparency of supply chain.

Use-cases of blockchain in the supply chain include the vendor payments, inventory management, asset tracking, regulatory audit and data security. These are the few common cases in the supply chain where block chaining is implemented, however, blockchain can be applied over any sort of business or communication. Data security application of blockchain is most commonly used in banking and healthcare organization across the globe.

Real world applications of the blockchain in supply chain are described as follows;

Vendor payments

One of the best cases of the blockchain in the supply chain is vendor payment. The main problem of vendor payment is the delay in the payments. Generations of invoices, monitoring the submission of required details, leading to payment is a critical and time-consuming process. On that account; the solution to the problem is as follows:

- The process of vendor payment in supply chain can be either automated, partially automated or may support both conditions using the smart contract. You can automate the process of payment depending on the trusted, authentic invoice. Furthermore, you can automatically trigger the payment using the smart contract.
- The smart contract sets the rules to govern the transactions so it can be partially automated or fully automated, or it can depend on both.
- The smart contract is a digital agreement.
- Such contracts are executed automatically without requiring third parties.

The advantages of vendor payments

The advantages of the vendor payment are as follows:

- Reduces the cost by automating the overall process
- Reduces the delays by fully or partially automating the process.
- Process become faster and reduces dependencies.
- Safe contracts between vendor and customer.
- Tamper-proof audit trails.

Inventory Management/record management:

Implementation of the blockchain method for inventory or record management helps in securing the records of the corporate and private organizations as their main concern is always security & management. Blockchain helps to maintain and secure business records; preventing any unauthorized modification.

The case of blockchain in the supply chain is inventory management/record management. The concern is how to maintain a critical business record and ensure data is not tampered?

Solution

- **Decentralization of server:** There is no any centralized inventory data storage as the blockchain functions over distributed network. It eliminates the risk of data loss and single-point of failure.
- **Process tracking and reporting:** Data can be checked and verified throughout the process of inventory management. A blockchain based on record management that generates unique digital signature of the business records and publishes them into the blockchain. This can be verified in any record whether it has been tampered or not.
- **Highly secured data:** In inventory management records, data entries are carried out on the blockchain that is encrypted, making it possible to forge data.
- **Anti-opaqueness:** It is fully immutable and all the parties include an access to a data file.
- **Data accuracy:** As we know, blockchain offers transparent ledger where each block is comprised from the previous block. Modification in any block is not possible. Similarly, each transaction contains statement of source and destination, which helps to avoid double spending.

The advantages of inventory management

The advantages of the inventory management are as follows;

- Independent of any authority for data verification.
- It is makes the process more trustable, transparent and reliable.
- Everyone can read the record, but only authorized users can write the record to make it completely safe and secured.

Asset Tracking

Supply chain is a huge process. It is very difficult of track the assets through a complete process of supply chain for an organization. The problem of asset tracking can be resolved by using blockchain. Blockchain ensures the entire supply chain process where purchase, delivery and dumping of any asset will be record in transactions. Nodes in the blockchain network can easily validate these transaction, making it very easy to track assets with block chaining.

The solution of the asset tracking is as follows:

- A blockchain is based on asset tracking system or inventory/record management.
- When the material is purchased, sold and consumed, they will all be tracked properly to the inventory management directly. Hence, whenever the material is purchased or blocked into the company or the branch, it will be initialized or created into the blockchain as digital assets.
- Whoever issues the materials or parts to a particular branch, it will be transferred to that person's account.
- Whenever the material is being consumed, they can be deleted from the blockchain or transferred to the consumed account.
- Challans, invoice, receipts are digitally stored and tracked in the blockchain.

The advantages of Asset Tracking

The advantages of the asset tracking are as follows:

- Tamper-proof audit trails ensure the visibility of the particular supply chain material inventory.
- Tracking of each asset.
- Tampering cannot go unnoticed.
- No need of reconciliation because of distributed ledger.

Regulatory Audit & Security

The problem of regulatory audit and security is ensuring the security of critical information. Blockchain can also be used in the authentication system, verification of confidential and critical information or simply in blockchain-based data verification systems.

The solution of regulatory audit and security are as follows;

- Blockchain-based on data verification and authentication system improves the security and transparency of the identity & access management processes including data verification system. The transparency in data verification using block chain is the best approach that ensures the reliability and authenticity. It is impossible to achieve this transparency in data security without the blockchain system.
- It also reduces the cost involved implementing the data security. Other solutions in data security require several hardware and software implementation adding additional layers of security.
- Any type of data that is signed or unsigned can be published into the blockchain, this can be easily noticed and verified by the users.
- Anyone can verify the data's authenticity & integrity at the time of retrieval.
- All the records will create or initialize the tamper-proof audit trails for the administrative or regulatory audit.

The advantages of Regulatory Audit & Security

The advantages of regulatory audit & security are as follows;

- No interaction required with official staff for data verification.
- Any data corruption will be instantly identified and mitigated.

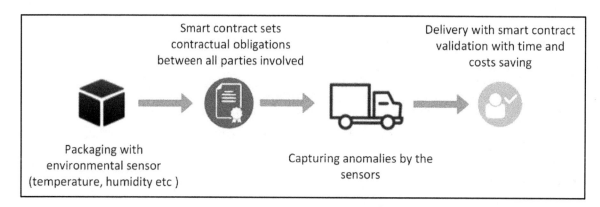

Figure 4-01: Blockchain use case supply chain

Healthcare Record Keeping

Healthcare record keeping is an important legislation defined in Human Rights Act 1998 and Data Protection Act 1998. It is neccessary to maintain and secure the health records not only for medical purposes such as compiling a complete record of patient's treatment but it is also required in legal & forensic cases. Healthcare industry requires a much more efficient, safe and secured system for healthcare payment, health record management, faster claim settlement, regulatory audit, and clinical trails' record keeping.

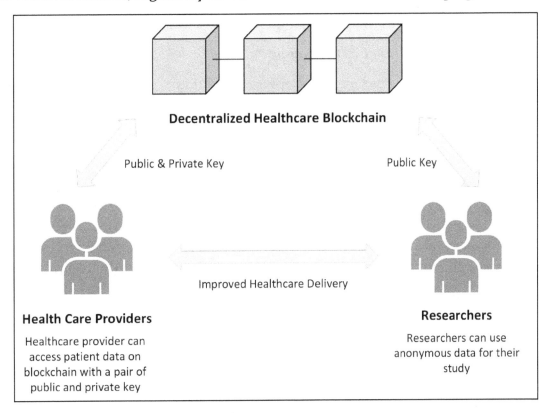

Figure 4-02: Healthcare in the blockchain

Some of the essential applications of healthcare are described as follows:

Health Record Management

Most of the hospitals see to maintain the patient's health record in a secured way. Using Blockchain, data is not only secured, it also detects if any record has been tampered with. Doctors and researchers accessing the data can verify the records and continue their work. If any information has been tampered with, it will be detected.

- Health industry can implement health record management with blockchain as a primary tool to maintain and keep the health records in a proper way and to ensure that the data has not been corrupted or tampered.
- Unique digital signatures of health records are stored in blockchain based health record management system.
- Patient and hospital can use APIs to verify whether their report has been tampered or not.
- Tampering cannot go unnoticed leading to the safety of the patients.
- Record sequenced information is saved in the blockchain.

The advantages of health record management

The advantages of health record management are as follows:

- Reduces the requirement of staff in a hospital for data verification.
- Is more trustable, transparent and reliable.
- Researchers, patients, doctors or anyone can read the record, but only authorized entities can write the record, making it completely safe and secured.

Electronic Medical Record

The electronic medical record is presently maintained in the data center, and the access is limited to hospitals and care provider networks. Blockchain handles the complete medical history for each patient with various granularities of control by the patients, hospitals, regulators, and doctors. It is providing a safe and secured mechanism to record and maintain a comprehensive medical overview of each patient.

The advantages of electronic medical record

The advantages of electronic medical record are as follows;

- Time reduced in insurance claims resolution and gained efficiency in providing insurance quotes.
- Tamper-proof means of storing medical histories.
- Complete patient medical history of drug recommendations by physicians.

Hospital Supply Tracking & Tracing

In a hospital, there are a lot of resources, assets and products that are being purchased and dumped on daily basis. These inventories of a hospital can't be traced easily. It will be a costly process without blockchain to trace the supply chain process in a hospital where a lot of medical resources are being used daily.

- Blockchain-based on inventory management and tracking system helps to track the resources in a hospital.
- Material purchased will initialize the process of blockchain.
- Issuing any asset to a particular account holder i.e. staff/doctor/manager, the transaction is recorded, hence can be easily verified.
- Whenever the material is consumed, it can be deleted from the blockchain or transferred to the consumed account.
- Challans, invoice, receipts are digitally stored and tracked in the blockchain.

The advantages of hospital supply tracking and tracing

The advantages of hospital supply tracking and tracing are as follows:

- Hospitals can track each material with at a fraction of the cost of the current system.
- No tampering
- No reconciliations required since everyone will be using the same ledger.
- Tamper-proof audit trails for administrative and regulatory requirement as there are some sensitive materials that are being issued to the hospital by the government on a regulatory basis.

Drugs tracking

In blockchain, drug tracking is another opportunity as it is the leveraging of the blockchain to develop tracking and chaining of custody from the manufacturer to the patient. Decentralization of trust and authority built the concept behind the technology over the traditional. This is the benefit of blockchain in drug tracking.

Devices tracking

In blockchain, device tracking is another opportunity in healthcare. Status of devices can be traced with the manufacturer's comments till decommissioning. The immutability and tamper-proof qualities of the blockchain are the advantages of blockchain device tracking over traditional.

Faster Claim Settlement

A typical process of claim settlement includes a lot of back and forth communication between parties included for the claim processing. One of the challenges faced during claim settlement is the payment processing action that can be reduced with the blockchain system. The blockchain solution can automate the needed workflow and can share a single copy of the contract to all the parties.

- Healthcare related payments are required for settlement, invoice, automated payment to the vendor, and healthcare insurance based payment can all be fully tracked and automated.
- Uses "smart contract" to automate payment process.
- Such a contractis executed automatically without the need of third parties.
- The smart contract sets the rules to govern the transactions so it can be partially automated or it can be fully automated, or it can depend on both.

The advantages of faster claim settlement

The advantages of faster claim settlement are as follows;

- Claims can be reviewed and paid more efficiently and quickly.
- The systems can suggest alternative services that have better coverage.
- Process becomes faster and reduces dependencies on employees.
- Reduces costs and delays associated with traditional contracts enforcement and pay-out process.
- Creates tamper-proof audit trails for administrative or regulatory auditor.

Administrative & Regulatory Audit

Insurance companies as well as the healthcare industry are very careful about the safety and security of the records. Responsible authorities will always want to ensure if any information is being altered. Blockchain is the best solution for administrative records and regulatory audit records.

- Blockchain-based on data verification and authentication system has been already discussed earlier in this chapter.
- Any type of data that is signed or unsigned can be published into the blockchain. This data may be any sort of administrative document.

- All the records will create or initialize the tamper-proof audit trails for the administrative or regulatory audits.

The advantages of the Administrative & Regulatory Audit

The advantages of the administrative and regulatory audit are as follows:

- No interaction needed with hospital staff for data verification.
- Any data corruption will be instantly identified and mitigated.

Test Report Verification

- Blockchain-based medicines and test report verifications; sometimes, legal matters require the verification of test reports. This legal matter based verification is very critical. Hence, this criticality can be handled using the blockchain.
- Reports are published by labs into the blockchain without any human interruption along with tracking details.
- The patient can use her/his mobile to verify whether the report has been tampered or not.
- Attributes can be justified from the blockchain without trusting any of the hospital staff.

The advantages of test report verification

The advantages of test report verification are as follows;

- No interaction with hospital staff for data verification.
- Anyone can read, but only authorized entities can write into the blockchain.

Clinical Trials Record keeping

Another blockchain technology use-case is the clinical trial record keeping. Records of a patient about its clinical trials are kept secured in blockchain. Consider a clinical record of a high-profile patient, any changes in the records may lead to wrong medication causing his death.

The Clinical record keeping method allows to secure the medical credentials of patients in a distributed ledger. It makes the verifiable information visible to trial recruiters and to reach out to the patients. Blockchain smart contract endorses the traceability and transparency over clinical trials arrangements.

- The most common issue of clinical trials is fraudulent trial or trials made by mistakes.
- Records are secured, transparent and authentic.
- Records can be securely allowed to be accessed and restricted to be modified.
- The collection of data may not be normalized or uniform.

Authentication and Modification

- All of the records are secured with a digital signature.
- Digitally signed records ensure the proof of existence, verification and transparency of trial data.
- Allows secured data sharing among researchers, communities, it also allows reproducibility.

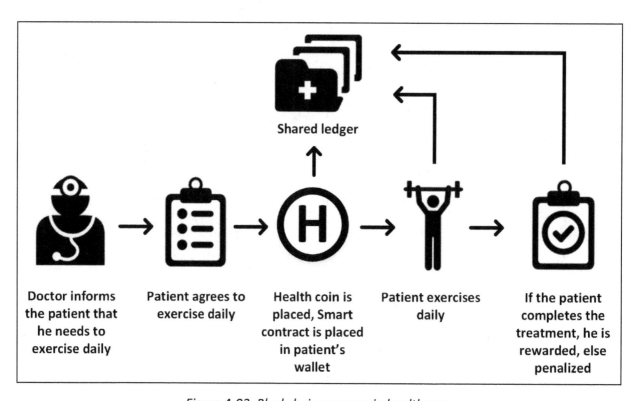

Figure 4-03: Blockchain use case in healthcare

Cyber Security

Cyber security is one of the essential use cases on the blockchain. Internet surfing has become a major security concern after the increase in cyber threats and identity theft over the last few years. It has become necessary to combat these cyber attackers in order to improve cyber security across the globe.

How blockchain can improve cyber security?

Blockchain has the potential to make the process transparent andsecure. It eliminates the risk of centralized network, tampering, modification, Denial-of-Service (DoS) attacks and much more. A 2017 IBM study of 3000 global C-suite executives found that 33 percent of organizations across a range of industries, are considering or using blockchain. Security fraud and cybercrime are the main reason of their interest.

Decentralized Storage – P2P Sharing

Storing records, data and files on a centralized location always gives a target to attackers to penetrate and steal the information. By storing this information on a decentralized location, hackers will now need millions of computers across the globe to be compromised. It is nearly impossible to compromise millions of computers all over the world, and then modify the blocks, though modifications have been noticed. Peer-to-peer sharing allows only authorized users to access the resources and modify them.

Blockchain may be played across the confidentiality, integrity, and availability. Offering improved resilience, auditing, transparency, and encryption.

There are many reasons why cyber security requires this technology; few are as follows:

- Overlapping coverage between provider's product
- Lack of incentive for security experts
- Lack of interoperability
- Centralized threat detection

The main benefits of cyber security on blockchain are as follows:

Confidentiality

Confidentiality defines the ability to avoid unauthorised parties to access any asset. Confidential assets are disclosed to authorised parties only. Confidentiality in a blockchain refers to the ability of any node in the network that transacts any digital asset without

disclosing this transaction with other nodes of the blockchain network. Confidentiality in a public blockchain is not so popular but applicable, as public blockchain is designed on the principle of transparency. Each transaction is publically available so that any entity can validate it. **Key Definition Function** (KDF) produces fresh key from Master key for each new transaction to enhance anonymity, however it is not enough to hide identity. Additionally, **Confidential Transaction** (CT) is used to ensure confidentiality in public blockchain. In CT, parties agree upon an encrypted value without disclosing these value to other entities. Furthermore, **Homomorphic Addition** provides additional layer of security to avoid revealing the amount.

Confidentiality in a private blockchain can be achieved by simply encrypting the blockchain data, it is called On-chain Encryption. This works by encrypting the transactions so that only intended participants can decrypt them. Additionally, centralizing the blockchain will allow the certain nodes to localize the data to prevent exposure. In such case, none of the participant will have full copy of the ledger. Some other techniques are **Zero-Knowledge Proof** and **Verifiable Secret Sharing** to maintain privacy.

Data Integrity

Keeping data consistency and guaranteeing integrity throughout its complete lifecycle is essential in information systems. Hash comparison, data encryption or the usage of digital signing are the samples of how system owners can satisfy the integrity of data, for all the stages it is in (transit, at rest or in use storage).

Hence, the blockchain makes characteristics, immutability, and traceability easier, producing organizations with a means to protect data integrity. This means that the distributed ledger makes sure the protection of data against destruction or modification. Apart from this, the technology protects the authenticity and irreversibility of full transactions. Encrypted block accommodates immutable data that is resistant to hacking.

This data integrity increases IoT and IIoT devices. For example, in a private blockchain, IBM produced its Watson IoT platform with the choice to conduct IoT data.

Cyber Fraud

One of the biggest reasons of access management and identity theft on the internet is the weak passwords. Accounts having weak password can be easily compromised. Password cracking of these accounts consumes less computation and time.

As we know, blockchain uses Public Key Infrastructure (PKI). Using public and private keys, blocks are hashed.Public key is broadcasted all over the network hence anyone can encrypt the data with the public key of recepient and send it. Recepieint will decrypt this data with the private key. It is used to create digital signature, a piece of code that helps guarantee that the author of a transaction is actually the individual who holds the private key. The digital signature along with the consistent public key help to specify the identity of the user who sent the transaction.

A public key infrastructure model eventually relies on the Central Authority (CA) to furnish, revoke and store key pairs. Key pair record handles the pairing of the private key with the public key.

The main problem is that CA is a centralized database. Compromising CA will compromise the entire security. Using blockchain, you can generate a distributed PKI model, by choosing CA to control and handle key pairs. Hence, you can save the data on the blockchain.

As far as hacking is concerned, it is simple to describe the malicious attitude to the P2P connections and distributed consensus. Now a day, blockchain are reflected as 'unhackable', an attacker can influence a network just by getting control of half the percent of the network nodes.

Right to be forgotten

Data privacy is essential to consider on how blockchain will fix side by side with data privacy law even if your information is immutable. How to execute the "*right to be forgotten*" in a technology which guarantees the users right of erasure of its data such as Personally Identifiable Information (PII)

As we know, blokchain is a decentralized ledger where all the transactions are publically available to be verified. This is the fundamental principle of blockchain technology where every new block created in the blockchain is associated with the previous one. To ensure the authenticity and transparency in blockchain, public and private keys are used, additionally, each block is hashed and associated with the previous block to assure that no one is able to modify or delete any value. This is the only princple that makes the

blockchain technology suitable to be used for financial transactions, and secured management processes.

One solution of this issue is to make sure all the information is encrypted enough that it cannot be decrypted without keys. An alternate solution to resolve this issue is by destroying the decryption key. Personal data i.e encrypted will be anonymized after the distruction of secret key. As a result, the blockchain technology protects the privacy of your information when you forget your key as no one else can decrypt it.

Data Quality

Blockchain technology does not guarantee or improve the quality of your data although public and private blockchain can guarantee the accuracy or quality of data. Encrypted data in the blockchain means that you can trust the data being drawn from organizations existing source system is of great quality, as in the case of all other blockchain technology systems.

Blockchain technology can play an important role in transforming data output as the technologies have original time capabilities, grant organizations to justify the transactional data quicker than any other system.

Decentralization

In decentralization, there is no requirement for any third party justification because of the peer to peer network, any user can recognize the network transactions. Blockchain users can trust the data in their blockchain network because the chain will not collapse. For example, if a person is not a part of blockchain (let us say an attacker), attempts to tamper a block, will require the tampering of the entire chain as each block is connected with the previous one. Any modification in a block will be noticed by the miners using consensus algorithms.

Tracking and Tracing

All transactions are either a public or a private blockchain. They are digitally signed and time stamped which means that the network user can trace back to the history of transactions and recognize the agreements. The blockchain can increase the reliability of the system (by detection of tampering) since each transaction is cryptographically associated with each other. From a cyber-security point of view, this provides entities proof that the data is authentic and has not been tampered with. This quality also permits companies to have authentic information about product distributions and assets.

Sustainability

Blockchain technology eliminates the single point of failure. It means that, when a system is on the target of DDoS attacks, failure of a single node will not impact the entire blockchain. It is impossible to compromise and turn down all of the nodes across the globe at once. Distributed database of ledger saves the blockchain from DoS attacks.

Resilience

Peer-to-peer nature of the technology or decentralized nodes within a network protects data across the globe, increases the resiliency round-the-clock even if few nodes are under attack or offline, it will continue because of the distributed nature of this technology.

Network Access

There is no essential requirement to control network access as the blockchain technology permits anyone to access or play a role in the network, provided that they have downloaded the software of public blockchain first. Appropriate security controls are needed to ensure network access in private blockchain. Administrators configure and deploy the blockchain network. They access the network to test and manage by using CLI.

- Blockchain applications then connect several nodes including CA, orderers, and peers.
- Blockchain administration and monitoring tools are used for managing and monitoring the services.

With public blockchains, anyone can participate in the network. Anyone can gain read-only role as well as make legit changes. These legit changes include adding a new block into the blockchain. Such blockchains are public, or un-permissioned blockchains.

Permissioned blockchain requires special permission to access, read, and write the information. Each participant can only contribute as authorized or defined in his/her role. Such blockchains are called permissioned blockchains.

Protected Communication

Distributed nature of ledger increases the protection of information from being tampered and modified. Numbers of miners across the network are continuously validating the transactions. It is not possible to hide any sort of tampering within a blockchain. Hashes are encrypted using public and private keys making them more difficult to decrypt.

Digital marketing

Digital marketing is a great field. Digital marketing has an important role in any business. In the U.S, companies are on the speed to spend almost $120 billion in digital marketing by 2021, creating one of the largest fields for businesses looking to market their brands. This makes them more visible in today's' diverse society. Digital marketing is growing day by day. Another technology that is advancing rapidly is blockchain, it is set to change the world of digital marketing in a new technique.

Blockchain aims to gain transparency in all sectors of businesses as the data is stored digitally and cannot be deleted or tampered.

The main benefits of digital marketing are as follows:

Editing

In blockchain, marketers can work collectively on a writing project with the capability to look when an edit is being made, where or who is making it. The file will be decentralized, meaning that no singular user has the complete ownership of that specific project.

Cloud-based and Google Docs platform have taken care of half the collection of this equation, but the problem of centrality and tracking still requires to be addressed. For example, CryptPad has started the process of integrating blockchain technology into editing and writing programs to pickup.

The capacity of blockchain to change the technique that we collect on written marketing projects is large.

Smart contract

- If you are in marketing, you will be considered to hire a contractor.
- A contractor is usually hired for a particular job description or to fulfill certain tasks such as, photography, scripting, designing, etc.
- Smart Contract can maintain the track of terms and conditions of the agreement.
- Basically, in the digital space, marketers take advantage from this blockchain application in many techniques. For example, in terms of ad enforcement, marketers can outline a smart contract, breaking down the terms of confirmation between a company and a publisher.
- Smart contracts can also be used to buy or authorize principle from content creators.

- Recently, Kodak introduced that they are working with a company to provide a blockchain-based service that pays photographers whenever a company separately uses their images.

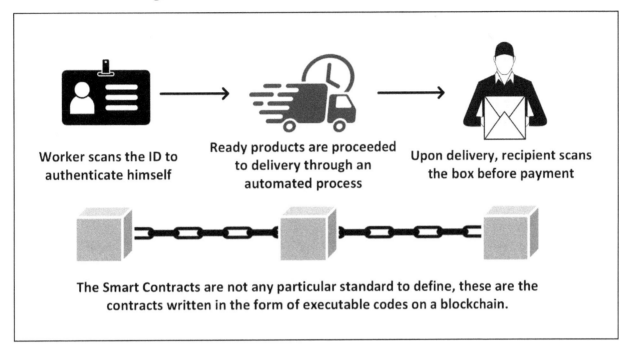

Figure 4-04: Smart Contract

Performance:

In performing, how a marketing campaign performs is always more essential than the time spent on it, but performance is very hard to track. If a marketer needs information on the performance of a project or any conducts or changes that came out of it, it takes a lot of time and collection with intermediaries. Affiliates, ad networks, and more in-between that attach the producer of the content to its audience.

Lack of transparency can even make you vulnerable to fraud and other problems.

If each participant in the marketing campaign has a duplicate performance data, there will be no lack of certainty. As no one person is completely owning the information, there is no need to panic about tampering.

Land Ownership

Sweden is the country where you can find the implementation of blockchain on land registries. The country has alreday taken steps towards the next phase in digitizing and securing the documentation of land ownership with this high level technology. It is one of the developed countries, working on advanced technologies; Property or land ownership is a major problem all over the world. There are numbers of disputes that arise on daily basis claiming for land ownership. There is a need of well-developed, secured and transparent land registries that can verify the legitimate owership, is secured enough to be trusted, and can clear misunderstandings among disputants. This transparency does not only authenticate the legitmate ownership but it also adds the transparency in the process and eliminates the resistance claiming for inheritance. The Swedish advancement in digitizing land registry is a revolution.

The Swedish system works on a private blockchain with the combination of land authorities and clients, holding copies of the records. Once a land ownership changes, each step of the process is recorded and can be verified on the blockchain. The system acts as a highly protected and secured service with transparent verification system for property transactions.

If the land registry information is missing, including registrations documents, It may becausesome part of the registration process gone wrong. It usually takes a longer time from purchasing contract till transfer of ownership.

To better understanding this case, we can review the main issues to address in the current processes;

- The issues above have resulted in sellers, purchasers, bank and real estate agents forced to create their complex processes for agreements since they have to verify that the process cannot go wrong.
- Registering a real estate transactions system is slow. The time between signing a legally binding purchasing contract and when the land registration authority receives the bill of sale, then making the approval of the title is frequently three to six months.
- Land registration authority has involved in some steps at the end of the real estate transactions. The majority of the process is not transparent and visible to the public or other stakeholders.

Solution:

The improving process associated is the solution that provides value to the real estate transaction and land transaction.

- The need for physical archives of files and contracts that are eliminating
- Flexibility & scalability in terms of increasing residence
- Greater security for users of the system
- Faster and more transparent transactions

Blockchain land registry process is for faster and transparent transactions, for increasing residence, for enhancing the security and for eliminating the physical storage and other paper work such as the traditional registration processes.

A blockchain is a digital registry that cannot be tampered. It delivers a mechanism for many parties to agree on a set of pre-defined rules (smart contracts). It prevents those parties from making fake statements since everyone can validate the transactions; it also prevents the alteration of statements after the addition of a block.

However, while bitcoin is the example of a public blockchain where all transactions are open to the public, financial and other institutions are trying to build private blockchains, where some data is available only to specific participants.

Bitcoin is the only way for a seller to transfer a unique piece of digital property (ownership) to a buyer, such that the transfer is guaranteed to be secured and safe. Everyone knows that the transfer has taken place and no one can challenge the legitimacy of the transfer. The significances of this development are hard to overstate.

We cannot rely on traditional technology, there is still a need to digitize real estate transactions.

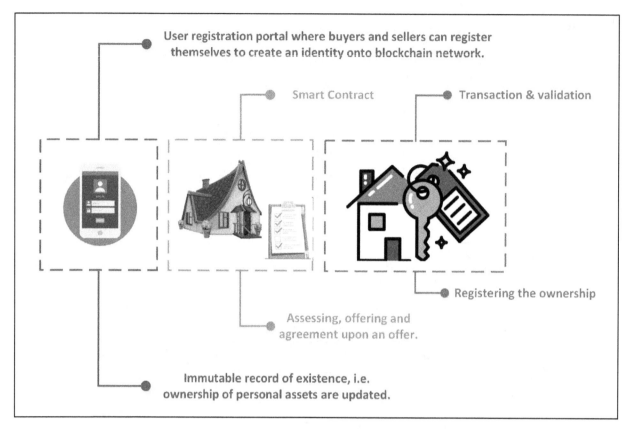

Figure 4-05: Working of Land Ownership

This diagram shows how the system workes when a real transaction has occurred. It also shows how each component operates with other components and makes a system that is capable, reliable, and secured, with less paperwork and transparent transactions. It increases the residence due to a more significant number of lands purchasing through this system.

Conclusion:

The blockchain is the part where the transparent transactions are recorded and stored. It is equivalent to the distributed ledger. The nodes decide what is going to be committed to the blockchain. There may also be nodes that are not part of the validation process but can still store the record.

The blockchain based property ownership recording system described in this use case eliminates most potential failures and attacks through transparency and use of cryptographic primitives for authentication. Thus, it can be used to reduce reliance on trusted third parties, reduce costs and the number of fraud and errors.

Finance Industry

The blockchain is the only essential technology in the finance sector since the advent of money and on how it modified the world. Few of the advantages of this new technology are; cost saving, faster transactions, decentralization, reliability, simplification, transparency, traceability, and improved data quality.

Fake Transaction

Latest reports indicate that about 45% of financial institutions such as stock exchange and money transfers suffer from economic crime yearly. A majority of organizations operate on a centralized database. A centralized database is vulnerable to cyber-attacks because it has a single point of failure where once a hacker breaches, he can get complete access to data in the system.

The blockchain is a shared digital ledger that approves recording and electronic verification of transactions through a network of computers in the absence of a central ledger. It resolves the problem of a vulnerable centralized database by presenting a decentralized database.

Capital Market

Usually, new industries have to focus on investors for necessary funding in their startup days.. The funding pattern changes in the advent of venture capitalists and then arrive the IPOs (Initial Public Offering) through a stock exchange which is a more advantageous route for self-established businesses. Nearly all these forms of fundraising are infested with many intermediaries including exchange operators, investment bankers, lawyers, auditors, and crowd-funding platforms.

Blockchain technology is transforming the equation by permitting businesses in spite of its size to increase funds on a peer-to-peer platform over shared offerings that is distributed globally. The startup industry is already under transformation by this new funding mechanism. In 2016, Blockchain companies were able to raise approximately $400 million from traditional venture capital investors and approximately $200 million through ICOs (Initial Coin Offerings).

Globally Connected Capital Market

Now days, the trading environment or capital market is more complex and faster. When you depends on trading partners, you cannot afford to have connectivity issues.. Blockchain system delivers Financial Markets Network services for voice, data and enterprise

connectivity. It can help your firm trade more rapidly, become more agile, and improve competitive advantages.

Financial Markets and Network Managed Network-as-a-Service (NaaS) have connected to a global network through the blockchain system that is connected to more than six thousand capital market participants around the globe. Throughout the trade lifecycle, you can quickly and easily reach anyone you need; buy-side and sell-side firms, trading platforms, market centers, trading platforms, interdealer brokers, liquidity venues, market data providers, and application settlement/clearing services.

Data Connectivity that is Fast and Reliable

We are trading diverse markets and using strategies that are more complex than ever. The number of data we deal with is enormous. Time spent managing numerous data feeds and various suppliers is so huge that we do not focus on what is the most important; driving profitability and serving our clients.

The blockchain system Network-as-a-Service (NaaS) solutions help us to have a fast, reliable data connectivity to all aspects of the trade lifecycle that are to order creation, placement, clearing, trade execution, reporting, settlement, and market data delivery. It helps us to stop spending time managing multiple suppliers. With an exclusive focus on the capital markets, the blockchain system delivers expertise and solutions that can help your firm become more efficient, productive and profitable.

Use Case:

User A and B are matched on an implementation site, and certainly, have verified that the other has the means to complete the transaction.

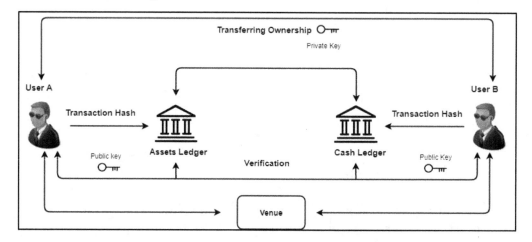

Figure 4-06: Transferring ownership through the entire system

User A demonstrably owns the security on the asset ledger, and User B demonstrably owns cash on the cash ledger. User A and B jointly sign the transaction by applying their private keys to unlock their cash or asset, and then by transferring ownership to the recipient via their public key. The signed transaction is broadcasted to the distributed ledger to validate and record in the next update, along with a contemporary update to a cash ledger.

Digital Identity

Digital identity is the common name given to an account's profile info, corresponding to the private masterkey that belongs to a user. Every profile has a unique identifier known as Digital Identity (DID). It is similar to an alias in Bitshares in Metaverse. Digital identity roles of ordinary users are any identity that can be applied to a typical user. They can participate in a system or applications using their digital identities.

Use Case:

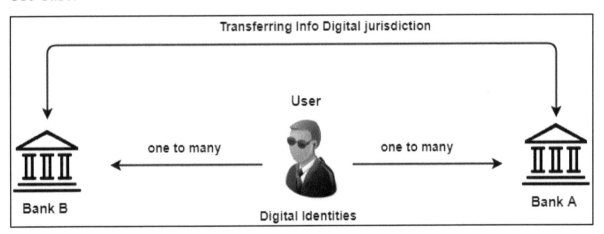

Figure4-07: Digital Identity

If a person possesses multiple digital identities and wants to open an account at Bank B, he will have to specify that he already has an account at Bank A. Because of this, Bank B can authorize him to open an account at their financial institution. This use case can be replicated at multiple financial institutions within the same legal jurisdiction.

Digital identity is also applicable in the field of digital rights. Digital assets that have been issued by a digital identity and possess multiple credentials are more valuable in the market, thus facilitating the transfer of different types of value other than the encrypted digital currencies. End users are able to use their digital identity to claim other assets and copyrights. Distant from authorizing certification information, users can also authorize others to access their private data such as credit data and reputation.

Metaverse

It's objectives are to deliver secure and convenient infrastructure services that rely on blockchain technology for a wide range of users, including corporations, individuals, and government institutions. It contains three pillars; Digital Assets, Digital Identities, and Value Intermediaries. It intends to build a web of smart properties. Metaverse follows the object-oriented programming paradigm that users can easily use on smart networks. These three pillars support all decentralized applications at the protocol level on Metaverse.

Types of Metaverse:

Metaverse has three type of ledgers:

- Digital asset ledgers
- Digital identity ledgers
- Data-feed ledgers

Like the digital asset ledgers in Metaverse, the architecture of digital identity ledgers is based on ETP transaction implementation.

The functions of digital identities contain identity verification and operation authorization.

The Functional Procedure of Digital Identities:

Authorization

To clarify the situations, we require authorization; authorization is often related to transactions. Let us suppose that A requests to inspect B's digital identity information.

Asset information is needed before providing any services. There are two possibilities;

1. B has massive amounts of assets on-chain, more than 1 million ETP. B can disclose his asset information to A.

2. B has some on-chain assets and various off-chain assets. With the old method, B will have to change the assets to ETP for authorization Now, Metaverse recommends that users issue their assets and get them verified, after which, they are registered as valid assets concerning one's digital identity.

A sends a request to B which generates a script that verifies the asset information of the targeted account, then sends A the encrypted result back. B is not capable of knowing which result contains information corresponding to the asset verification. Additionally, the initial request is also encrypted. Therefore, B does not know the specific request of A, but only the information which was requested. Personal transaction and asset records can be

accessed after the permission has been given on-chain, but the basic principle remains unchanged.

Personally customized fields are similar to assets that undergo Oracle authentication (information that has not been approved by an Oracle can still be authorized, but it is not recommended).

If the personal customized field has non-public information such as phone numbers and mailbox, the information is certified as same as schooling records.

Authentication process:

The authentication of personally customized information:

A system data-feed is used for endorsement. A system is presented as a third party and publishes all profiles on the blockchain for public inquiry and supervision.

Firstly, B fills in the customizable field with information that needs to be proven. Then, the System must use its master private key to sign the information and employ a larger sum of coin days to endorse it.

"A" can request the field's information (including the system endorsement) on a chain.

"A" can continue to provide services to B if A is convinced that B's information is valid.

Verification

Profiles can deliver effective chains of proof that demonstrate objective facts of any specified digital identity. On behalf of users, they first need to prove that a digital identity belongs to them by binding the transaction to the digital identities (the transaction domain contains DID information).

Creation

Each user can create a digital identity and bind it with his or her master private key.

If a user makes a digital identity but does not bind it to any master private key, this DID is regarded as an unauthenticated account and is notable to give access to some of its applications or functionalities.

Those who have registered their assets is a Master Private Key holder that is on behalf of the Metaverse blockchain. They can also select not to bind any digital identities. Users need to take the initiative because Metaverse does not automatically generate digital identities for any user. The decision to combine a DID lies with the master private key's holder.

How the System works

- Users with data must establish his or her digital identity on Metaverse, provide data with the user-defined format, and submit this data to a system that is responsible for data authentication and endorsement.
- Systems (a digital identity) qualified to endorse data verify the validity and authenticity of the submitted data;
- After its owner and a system sign the data, it is binded with the owner's digital identity through master private keys.
- More users can view detailed information about this data after the data's owner gives his/her authorization.

Conclusion

Metaverse continues to advance its digital identity system and expand appropriate infrastructure services to engage more third-party designers to build applications based on the blockchain Metaverse, increasing the use of our Wallet which is an easy identity management service for ordinary users.

Cross-border Payments

The transfer of value across-borders whether it is payments or goods is always a slow and expensive process.

Use Case:

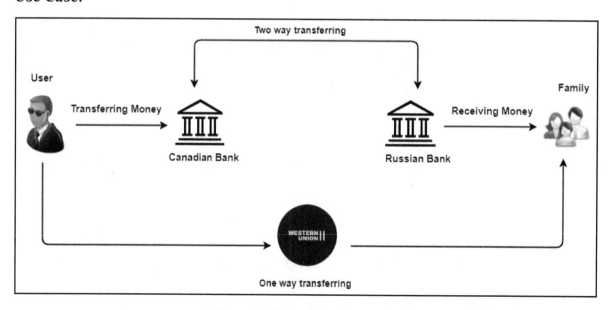

Figure 4-08: Cross Border Payment

If a person wishes to transfer money from Canada to their family in Russia, they have to have an account with a local financial institution. It takes some financial institutions and currencies before the money can be collected. A person can use services like Western Union for the same transaction which is faster but very expensive.

High Speed and Reasonable

The blockchain can speed up, simplify, and reduce the costs significantly. Blockchain can simplify this process and speed it up, cutting out many of the traditional intermediaries. At the same time, it makes money remittance more affordable. So far, the costs of remittance were 5-20%. A blockchain reduces the costs to 2-3% of the total amount and provides guaranteed, real-time transactions across borders.

Problems in the System:

Blockchain technology is gaining success in the field of money remittance. Certainly, there are some problems to consider. The most critical problem in this system is the lack of regulation for cryptocurrencies. If money is transferred from one country to another using blockchain technology wallet, and one of the wallet providers goes bankrupt, or hackers attack the wallet, the cryptocurrency stored is lost, then there is no central authority similar to a bank to reimburse the loss.

Exchange in the Cryptocurrency:

It is the same as the problem of exchanging the cryptocurrency back into locally accepted "fiat money" at the destination.

"The government has declared to legalize tender that states currency as Fiat money, but physical commodity does not back it. The value of fiat money is derived from the relationship between demand and supply rather than the worth of the material from which the money has been made."

It often requires the use of a cryptocurrency exchanger where currencies such as Bitcoin are traded for US dollars.

An exchange can increase extra complexity and runs the risk of fluctuating exchange rates, this can be extreme for cryptocurrencies. However, various people are willing to take these risks, as the advantages outweigh the drawbacks. Their numbers have the potential to go up once more beneficial regulations have been developed.

Regulators

When regulation is implemented, blockchain technology also has an exciting option for cross-border corporate payments. It is challenging as individual clients can loose their money when parties go bankrupt, and even more disturbing for corporates transferring enormous amounts of money through cross-border payments. With the proper regulation, financial institutions can be able to offer their corporate clients exciting propositions relying on blockchain technology. They are already developing their understanding of blockchain technology and developing proofs of the concept.

Globalization

On a worldwide scale, more countries are improving regulation in the field of cryptocurrency, as they acknowledge its importance for an innovative climate.

Testing

Though the advantages of cryptocurrencies and other blockchain technology applications have become clear in the last few years of startups, financial institutions are actively testing with blockchain technology and pressing regulators for action. Even in DNB itself, people are experimenting internally to become more familiar with cryptocurrencies in the form of a 'DNB-coin'. More transparent rules for financial institutions, corporates and individuals are only a matter of time.

Loyalty and Reward

A customer loyalty program permits companies to attract new clients and offer them special discounts and deals. The programs typically rely on a point system, in which a program member earns points on purchases that can be redeemed on exceptional deals. Loyalty programs can have various organizations as partners to serve a client base. For customers managing an array of loyalty programs, blockchain delivers instant redemption and exchange for several loyalty point currencies on a single platform. In just a single digital "wallet" of points, customers do not have to hunt for each program's options, limitations, and redemption rules.

System or Application

Using Hyperledger to develop a customer loyalty program with blockchain, the system allows members to register on the network and sign in to perform transactions. Members are able to view the partners on the network and perform transactions with them. These

transactions include earning points on purchases and redeeming those points on deals. Members are able to view all their transactions as a part of the blockchain ledger.

Partners get registered on the network through the application. To view the transactions associated with them, they have to sign in to their account. Dashboard displays statistics and total points allocated and redeemed.

This kind of pattern is used for the person who develops the system, and the person who is looking to start building blockchain applications with Hyperledger. When the person completes this pattern, the customer will understand how the system works.

- Develop a simple business network using Hyperledger.
- An instance of Hyperledger Fabric deploys the network locally.
- Build a system to interact with the blockchain network.

Use Case:

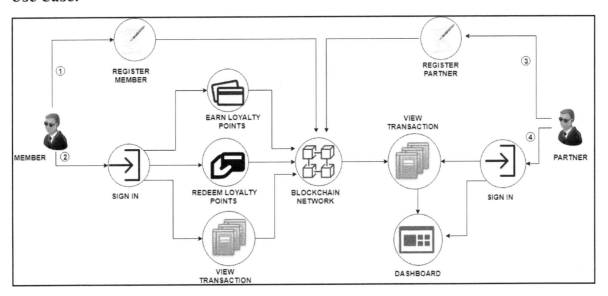

Figure 4-09: Loyalty and Reward

This diagram shows how the overall system works using a blockchain network.

- In the network, a member is registered.
- The member can sign in to create transactions to earn points, redeem points, and view transactions.
- In the network, a partner is registered.
- The partner can sign in to view transactions and display dashboard.

Conclusion:

The Blockchain technology presents various opportunities that transform the financial sector. The blockchain is exponentially opening up worldwide markets in similar ways as the internet revolutionized access to information. It's potential has no barriers; consumers, in addition to entrepreneurs, can accomplish access to every service or assets they require wherever they are and whenever they require them.

Practice Questions

1. What is the fundamental principal of blockchain technology?
    A. It is a decentralized distributed database of immutable records.
    B. It is a centralized distributed database of immutable records.

2. Who is the founder of Bitcoin?
    A. Vitalik Buterin
    B. Satoshi Nakamoto

3. Who is the founder of Ethereum?
    A. Vitalik Buterin
    B. Satoshi Nakamoto

4. Which algorithm is used in Bitcoin for creating bitcoin address?
    A. AES
    B. SHA-128
    C. SHA-256
    D. RSA

5. What are the two types of record in blockchain database?
    A. Block record
    B. Miner record
    C. Transactional record

    D. Consensus record

6. Each block consists of?
   A. Time Stamp
   B. Hash Pointer
   C. Transactions
   D. All of the above
   E. None of the above

7. A block in blockchain support _____ parent block(s).
   A. 1
   B. 2
   C. 3
   D. 4

8. Which of the following are consensus algorithms?
   A. PBFT (Practical Byzantine Fault Tolerance)
   B. Proof-of-Work
   C. Proof-of-Stake
   D. Delegated Proof-of-Stake
   E. Proof-of-Elapsed time
   F. All of the above
   G. None of the above

9. How many types of blockchain are there?
   A. 1
   B. 2
   C. 3
   D. 4

10. Which type of record can a blockchain can store?
    A. Health record

B. Business transactions

C. Management records

D. Financial records

E. All of the above

F. None of the above

11. A set of protocols which validates, exchange shares, money, or enforce the negotiation without a centralized organization is called?

A. Smart Contracts

B. Minting

C. Distributed Ledger

D. Token

12. Which technology is use to digitize a real estate transaction?

A. Traditional technology

B. Blockchain advance technology

13. How many copies of the contract, a system sent?

A. 2

B. 3

C. 4

D. 5

14. Which entities save the copy of the contract of sold land?

A. Purchaser, Seller, Bank

B. Purchaser, Seller, System

C. Purchaser, Seller, Seller Bank

D. Purchaser, Seller, Agent

15. How many e-paper has signed when land is sold?

A. 3

B. 4

C. 5

D. 6

16. Which master key is used in Digital Identity?

A. Private master key

B. Public master key

17. How much percentage can reduce the blockchain while using a cross-border payment method?

A. 1-2%

B. 2-3%

C. 3-4%

D. 4-5%

18. Which type of customer can attract to a customer loyalty program?

A. Old customer

B. Exciting customer

C. New Customer

19. Which algorithm is used in Bitcoin for mining?

A. AES

B. SHA-128

C. SHA-256

D. RSA

20. How does a block is recognized in the Blockchain?

A. Nonce

B. Hash Pointer

C. Hash

D. Block ID

21. What is Double Spending?
    A. Spending a digital token multiple times
    B. Fake transactions
    C. Multiple transactions

22. Name the common type of ledgers in blockchain network?
    A. Centralized Ledgers
    B. Decentralized Ledgers
    C. Distributed Ledgers
    D. All of the above

23. Which of the following is the application of Blockchain platform "*Ripple*"?
    A. Digital Currency
    B. Cross-border payments
    C. Logistics
    D. Voting

24. Which of the following Consensus algorithm is used in "*NEO*"?
    A. Proof-of-Work
    B. Delegated Byzantine Fault Tolerance (dBFT)
    C. Loopchain Fault Tolerance(LFT)
    D. Delegated Proof of Stake

25. What is the document proposed as "must read" for bitcoin?
    A. The Bitcoin Manifesto
    B. The Bitcoin White Paper
    C. The Bitcoin Constitution
    D. Bitcoin and the Blockchain

26. Which bitcoin exchange in Japan was hacked in 2014?
    A. Tradehill
    B. Bit Tradde

C. Bitstamp

D. Mt.Gox

27. How many botcoins will ever be created?

A. 210000

B. 2100000

C. 21000000

D. Unlimited

28. You can send a bitcoin on Ethereum address:

A. True

B. False

29. The nodes which creates new blocks are called?

A. Account holders

B. Miners

C. Verifiers

D. Mitigators

30. The central server of Bitcoin is located at:

A. Washington DC

B. Japan

C. Undisclosed Location

D. No central server

31. What information does a wallet contain?

A. Key pairs for each of your addresses

B. Transactions done from/to your addresses

C. Default key

D. Reserve keys

E. Version Number

F. All of the above

G. None of the above

Answers:

Chapter 1: Blockchain Basics

1. D.

Explanation:

Blockchain was invented by Satoshi Nakamoto.

2. A, B.

Explanation:

The blockchain is a technology or a concept.

3. B.

Explanation:

The blockchain is decentralized ledger tracking digital assets on the P2P network.

4. C.

Explanation:

Decentralized nodes are being distributed among the multiple nodes.

5. D.

Explanation:

Bitcoin is an application, implementation or cryptocurrency.

6. C.

Explanation:

The transactions are connected to the user bitcoin's address that is stored on a general ledger called Blockchain.

7. B.

Explanation:

The concept of "Proof of work" is to build a bitcoin platform.

8. C.

Explanation:

Bitcoin is equal to toy golden unicorn.

9. B.

Explanation:

The smart contract is used to define the computer program code that is capable of the facility, executing and enforcing the negotiation or the performance of an agreement by using blockchain technology.

10. D.

Explanation:

High security, availability, verifiability and auditability, trustless are the benefits of using blockchain technology.

11. A, B, C, D, E.

Explanation:

Trade services, investment, payment, wealth management, securities are the application for cost saving and faster dealing

12. A.

Explanation:

There are two functions of the blockchain database

- Read
- Write

13. B.

Explanation:

There are four functions of the traditional blockchain

- Create
- Read

- Update
- Delete

14. B.

Explanation:

The process of recording the pending transaction by adding a new block into the blockchain through mathematical puzzle (proof of work) is called blockchain mining.

15. B.

Explanation:

Miner is referred to a computer or server that does all the required computation to guess a new block.

16. D.

Explanation:

Bitcoin, ethereum,and NEO are the applications of blockchain.

17. A.

Explanation:

There are two types of blockchain developer.

- Blockchain core developer
- Blockchain software developer

18. A.

Explanation:

ICO stands for Initial Coin Offering.

19. B.

Explanation:

There are three kinds of ethereum applications.

- Financial application
- Semi-financial application
- Nonfinancial application

20. A.

Explanation:

The application that is designed to find the rates between two digital assets and to make it trade crypto is called stellar's SDEX exchange.

Chapter 2: Blockchain Intermediate

1. B (Public and Private Key)

Explanation

Asymmetric encryption uses public and private keys to encrypt and decrypt data.

2. C (A key is not given to the public)

Explanation

It is a secret number that allows bitcoins to spent. Each an every Bitcoin wallet holds one or more private keys, which are saved in the wallet file.

3. D (A block reward)

Explanation

The incentive for dedicating computing resources to the network and continuously expending energy to verify transactions is the block reward and transaction fees.

4. D (Prevents double spending)

Explanation

It tries a different strategy for spending and prevents double spending with the same nonce. First A sends transaction Ao to B, and then it sends another transaction Ao to C.

5. A (A Decentralized Application)

Explanation

Decentralized applications (DAPP) are applications that run on a P2P network of computers rather than only one computer.

6. A (Mining)

Explanation

Asymmetric cryptography is a branch of cryptography where a secret key can divide into two parts, a public key, and a private key. While a passphrase is similar to a password because the password is generally referred to something used to authenticate or log into a system. A password generally refers to a secret used to protect an encryption key. When mining is not used in this type of scenario.

7. D (All of the above)

Explanation

Digital currencies are the well-known type of digital token.

Utility tokens give access to users to use a platform

The privacy-centric digital currency Monero (XMR) uses codes that allow transaction amounts.

8. C (On an exchange)

Explanation

Many investors buy a cryptocurrency from an exchange. However, like any other online entity, the exchanges are vulnerable to hacking.

9. C (Satoshi Nakamoto)

Explanation

The original inventor of Bitcoin is Satoshi Nakamoto.

10. D (Peer to Peer)

Explanation

Peer-to-Peer (P2P) represents the computers that participate in the network and are peers to each other.

11. B (A computer on a Blockchain network)

Explanation

A node can be an active electronic device, including a computer, phone or even a printer, as long as it is connected to the internet and has an IP address.

12. D (Floppy Disk)

Explanation

Cryptocurrency wallets are specific to the cryptocurrency that is stored inside them.

13. B (Computers that validate and process Blockchain transactions)

Explanation

Miners tend to invest in compelling computing devices known as CPUs (central processing units) or GPUs (graphics processing units).

14. B (All of the above)

Explanation

- Cryptocurrency exchanges (online)
- Bitcoin ATMs (you put money inside and can load your bitcoin wallet)
- Bitcoin Voucher Cards (i.e., Austrian Post office, House of Nakamoto, Azteco London)
- Buy it personally from other people

15. C (A peer to peer network on a distributed ledger)

Explanation

The blockchain is a decentralized distributed ledger on a peer-to-peer network, which maintains a continuously growing number of transactions and data records.

16. A (A fork)

Explanation

In a hard fork, ifone group of nodes continues to use the old software while the other nodes use the new software, a split can occur.

17. D (A paper wallet)

Explanation

Cold storage is an offline wallet delivered for storing bitcoins. A simple type of cold storage is a paper wallet.

18. A (The first block after each block)

Explanation

The first block of a blockchain is a genesis block. The latest versions of Bitcoin number it as block 0, though earlier versions counted it as block 1.

19. C (Gas)

Explanation

It can execute scripts using an international network of public nodes. Gas is an internal transaction pricing mechanism, it is used to mitigate spam and allocate resources on the network.

20. B (A transaction and block verification protocols)

Explanation

It is also a mechanism for confirming the transactions and placing a number of their coins on a block to confirm a transaction block.

Chapter 3: Blockchain Advanced

1. B. (Private Blockchain)

Explanation: Private blockchain is accessible only to those who have the permission from the authorized parties, it may be an individual or an organization.

2. A. (Public Blockchain)

Explanation: Public blockchain is a permissionless blockchain, anyone can easily gain access to them.

3. D. (All of the above)

Explanation: Only authorized nodes can read and write the ledger information.

4. C. (Miners)

Explanation: Keep a few things in mind while setup your own blockchain, you have to take care of miners and setup your own miners.

5. E. (All of the above)

Explanation: We can setup our own blockchain by using Ethereum, OpenChain, Multichain, Hyperledger fabric, and Bitcoin.

6. B. (Multichain)

Explanation: Multichain is an open source platform and is founded by Mr. Gideon Greenspan.

7. D. (Hyperledger fabric)

Explanation: Private blockchain can be created by Hyperledger fabric because it does not have the concept of Mining or Cryptocurrency.

8. A. (Hyperledger)

Explanation: Hyperledger is actually the project hosted by Linux foundation, umbrella and fabric is one of the project hosted under the Hyperledger project.

9. B. (Store large data)

Explanation: Blockchain is distributive in nature, hence it does not store large string of data. Therefore, blockchain is not useful in such cases.

10. C. (Share common database)

Explanation: When organizations need to share a common database across their employees, contractors, or third-parties, the permissioned blockchain can really fit into this situation.

11. B. (Defining the Goal)

Explanation: Blockchain building starts with an appropriate goal that it is beneficial for you.

12. D. (Integrate Upcoming Technologies)

Explanation: Blockchain solution can be integrated by emerging technologies to enhance its capability like Artificial Intelligence, Biometrics, Cloud, Cognitive services, Internet of Things, Machine Learning.

13. C. (Designing the Admin-User Interface)

Explanation: Designing the Admin-User Interface is a separate step of building blockchain. It is not a part of building APIs.

14. D. (All of the above)

Explanation: Each block consists of a hash pointer to the previous block, timestamp, and list of transactions.

15. B. (More than one)

Explanation: Decentralized network has more than one parent node with many child nodes

16. D. (All of the above)

Explanation: All options are valid for decentralized network.

17. C. (Anyone can request for transaction)

Explanation: Blockchain processing begins with the person requesting for a transaction in the blockchain.

18. C. (Validation & Verification)

Explanation: These nodes validate the transaction and the user's status by using consensus mechanism.

19. A. (Creating a new block)

Explanation: When the transaction has been verified by all the nodes of the network, it is combined with the existing transactions to create a new block of data for the ledger.

20. B. (Modified)

Explanation: Modified data is the most appropriate option.

21. C. (Transaction is Complete)

Explanation: The working of blockchain architecture completes the requested transaction making it a permanent part of the blockchain.

22. C. (Smart coding)

Explanation: Smart contract works smartly with smart programming code.

23. D. (Ethereum)

Explanation: Ethereum is the most preferred choice because it provides scalable processing capabilities.

24. C. (Distributed leger)

Explanation: Triggering an event occurs after the ledger is distributed among all the nodes.

25. A. (Previous block)

Explanation: In blockchain, blocks are linked with previous blocks as the paper of a book.

Chapter 4: Blockchain Use-Case

1. **A** (It is a decentralized distributed database of immutable records)

Explanation: In blockchain technology, digital information is distributed among peers all over the world, this information is distributed, not stored at any single location, all records are public and easily verifiable, since it is being distributed among thousands of machines block chaining is nothing but a ledger.

2. **B** (Satoshi Nakamoto)

Explanation: Blockchain was invented by Satoshi Nakamoto in 2008 to serve as the public transaction ledger of the cryptocurrency bitcoin.

3. **A** (Vitalik Buterin)

Explanation: Vitalik is the creator of Ethereum. He first discovered blockchain and cryptocurrency technologies through Bitcoin in 2011.

4. **C** (SHA-256)

Explanation: SHA-256 is used in the creation of bitcoin addresses to improve security and privacy.

5. **A, C** (Block & Transactional records)

Explanation: Two types of records in blockchain database are block records and transactional records. Both these records can easily be accessed, and the best thing is, it is possible to integrate them with each other without following the complex algorithms.

6. **D** (All of above)

Explanation: Each block consists of cryptographic hash of previous block, timestamp and transaction data.

7. **A** (1)

Explanation: Each block references a previous block, also known as the parent block, in the "previous block hash" field, in the block header.

8. **F** (All of the above)

Explanation: Following are the consensus algorithm

- PBFT (Practical Byzantine Fault Tolerance)
- Proof-of-work
- Proof-of-stake
- Delegated proof-of-stake
- Proof-of-elapsed time

9. **C** (3)

Explanation: There are three types of Blockchains:

- Public
- Private
- Consortium

10. **E** (All of the above)

Explanation: Blockchain can be implemented of any sort of ledger.

11. **A** (Smart Contracts)

Explanation: A smart contract is a computer protocol intended to digitally facilitate, verify, or enforce the negotiation or performance of a contract. Smart contracts allow the performance of credible transactions without third parties. These transactions are trackable and irreversible.

12. **B** (Advanced Technology)

Explanation: We cannot use traditional technology and continue to digitize real estate transactions. Advance digitization of the process could make a considerable difference. Everybody has established a reliable solution for creating, enacting, verifying, storing and securing digital contracts.

13. **C** (Four)

Explanation: The system sends four copies of the contract, one for the seller, for the Purchaser, for the agent and for the Purchaser's bank.

14. **D** (Purchaser, Seller, Agent)

Explanation: The Purchaser, Seller, as well as the agent, each saves a copy of the contract, as well as a copy for the Purchaser's bank, and the Purchaser may now move into the property.

15. **A** (Three)

Explanation: Seller has signed the bill of sale, transfer the possession of the property and make the final payment.

16. **A** (Private master key)

Explanation: Digital identity is the common name given to an account's profile info, corresponding to the private master key that belongs to a user.

17. **B** (2-3%)

Explanation: A blockchain reduces the costs to 2-3% of the total amount and provides guaranteed, real-time transactions across borders.

18. **C** (New Customer)

Explanation: A customer loyalty program permits companies to attract new clients and hold clients with special discounts and deals.

19. **C** (SHA-256)

Explanation: SHA-256 is used in several different parts of the Bitcoin network:

- Mining uses SHA-256 as the Proof of work algorithm.
- SHA-256 is used in the creation of bitcoin addresses to improve security and privacy.

20. **B** (Hash Pointer)

Explanation: Hash pointer of each block links with the previous block in a blockchain. Hash stored in the hash pointer is the hash of the whole data of the previous block.

21. **A** (Spending a digital token multiple times)

Explanation: It's a condition when one digital token is spent multiple times because the token generally consists of a digital file that can easily be cloned.

22. **D** (All of the above)

Explanation: There are three types of ledgers; Centralized, Decentralized and Distributed.

23. **B** (Cross-border Payments)

Explanation: Ripple is used for cross-border payments.

24. **B** (Delegated Byzantine Fault Tolerance (dBFT))

Explanation: Delegated Byzantine Fault Tolerance (dBFT) is used as consensus algorithm in NEO.

25. **B** (The Bitcoin Whitepaper)

Explanation: Satoshi authors and releases a white paper titled Bitcoin: A Peer-to-Peer Electronic Cash System. This document is referred as must read document to understand the concept of block chaining.

26. **D** (Mt. Gox)

Explanation: Mt. Gox was a bitcoin exchange based in Shibuya, Tokyo, Japan. The company issued a press release on February 10, 2014, stating that the issue was due to transaction malleability: "A bug in the bitcoin software makes it possible for someone to use the bitcoin network to alter transaction details to make it seem like a sending of bitcoins to a bitcoin wallet did not occur when in fact it did occur.

27. **C** (21,000,000)

Explanation: 21 Million is the maximum cap which is not yet fully mined.

28. **B** (False)

Explanation: You cannot send bitcoin directly to an Ethereum address.

29. **B** (Miners)

Explanation: Miners are the creator of new blocks in a blockchain.

30. **D** (No Central Server)

Explanation: Blockchain technology is depends upon decentralized network & distributed database.

31. **F** (All of the above)

Explanation: Wallet contain Wallet.dat file containing:

- Keypairs for each of your addresses
- Transactions done from/to your addresses
- User preferences
- Default key
- Reserve keys

- Accounts
- A version number
- Key pool
- Info about current chain

References

Blockchain Basics

https://gblogs.cisco.com/in/blockchain/

https://blockgeeks.com/guides/what-is-blockchain-technology/

https://talkingtech.cliffordchance.com/en/fintech/blockchain---what-it-is-and-why-it-s-important.html

https://www.pwc.com/m1/en/media-centre/articles/blockchain-new-tool-to-cut-costs.html

https://medium.com/@gaurangtorvekar/7-blockchain-technologies-to-watch-out-for-in-2017-4b3fc7a85707(hyperledger)

https://blog.indorse.io/11-blockchain-technologies-to-look-out-for-in-2018-13af946089a6(almost   all types)

https://blockchainhub.net/blockchains-and-distributed-ledger-technologies-in-general/

https://www.futuretechpodcast.com/podcasts/records-keeper-open-public-blockchain-record-keeping-data-security/

https://www.blockchain-council.org/cryptocurrency/what-is-hyperledger-technology/

https://github.com/ethereum/wiki/wiki/White-Paper#applications

https://www.stellar.org/how-it-works/stellar-basics/#how-it-works

https://cryptocurrencyfacts.com/what-is-stellar/

https://www.bitdegree.org/tutorials/what-is-eos/

https://www.altencalsoftlabs.com/blog/2017/02/blockchain-ultimate-relief-cybersecurity/

https://www.blockchain-council.org/blockchain/blockchain-different-database/

https://neonexchange.org/

https://www.stellar.org/blog/2018-Stellar-Roadmap/

https://blockgeeks.com/guides/what-is-blockchain-technology/

Blockchain Intermediate

https://medium.com/@mattdlockyer/understanding-blockchain-technology-2cb5636823eb

https://hackernoon.com/public-vs-private-blockchain-4b4aa9326168

https://blockchainhub.net/blockchains-and-distributed-ledger-technologies-in-general/

https://www.ibm.com/blogs/blockchain/2017/05/the-difference-between-public-and-private-blockchain/

https://www.safaribooksonline.com/library/view/mastering-bitcoin/9781491902639/ch06.html

https://www.quora.com/Is-blockchain-a-peer-to-peer-system

https://www.investopedia.com/terms/b/block-bitcoin-block.asp

https://programmingblockchain.gitbooks.io/programmingblockchain/content/bitcoin_transfer/transaction.html

https://www.blockchain-council.org/blockchain/can-blockchain-private-key-be-hacked/

https://unblock.net/what-is-a-blockchain-address/

https://www.ccn.com/bitcoin-transaction-really-works/

https://en.bitcoin.it/wiki/Satoshi_(unit)

https://www.blockchain-council.org/blockchain/what-is-pool-mining-how-it-works/

https://www.blockchain-council.org/blockchain/solo-mining-works/

https://blog.nem.io/what-are-poi-and-vesting/

https://cointelegraph.com/explained/proof-of-work-explained

https://medium.com/novamining/main-differences-between-pow-and-pos-cryptocurrency-mining-c4cc279d9739

https://steemit.com/bitcoin/@mooncryption/guide-proof-of-work-pow-vs-proof-of-stake-pos-vs-delegated-proof-of-stake-dpos

https://bitfalls.com/2018/04/24/whats-the-difference-between-proof-of-work-pow-proof-of-stake-pos-and-delegated-pos/

https://bitshares.org/technology/delegated-proof-of-stake-consensus/

https://lisk.io/academy/blockchain-basics/how-does-blockchain-work/delegated-proof-of-stake

https://delegatecall.com/questions/how-to-tell-the-difference-of-pow-pos-and-dpos-to-my-child2bd36f15-a428-42a4-835a-7ef9e1113f26

https://blockonomi.com/delegated-proof-of-stake/

https://www.smithandcrown.com/definition/proof-of-importance/

https://www.mycryptopedia.com/proof-of-importance/

https://cryptoslate.com/nem/

https://hackernoon.com/the-difference-between-traditional-and-delegated-proof-of-stake-36a3e3f25f7d

https://blog.nem.io/what-are-poi-and-vesting/

https://lisk.io/academy/blockchain-basics/benefits-of-blockchain/blockchain-security

https://www.newgenapps.com/blog/blockchain-security-how-safe-it-is

https://www.csoonline.com/article/3279006/blockchain/4-reasons-blockchain-could-improve-data-security.html

https://www.technologyreview.com/s/610836/how-secure-is-blockchain-really/

https://www.weforum.org/agenda/2018/04/how-secure-is-blockchain/

https://lisk.io/academy/blockchain-basics/benefits-of-blockchain/blockchain-security

https://www.huffingtonpost.in/raja-raman/blockchain-can-transform-the-world-but-is-it-fool-proof_a_21660586/

https://www.forbes.com/sites/jasonevangelho/2018/03/13/mining-101-what-exactly-is-cryptocurrency-mining/#23db654aa83a

Blockchain Advanced

https://www.safaribooksonline.com/library/view/hands-on-cybersecurity-with/9781788990189/11986eb3-9c9c-4758-964d-226bd331980d.xhtml

https://www.entrepreneur.com/article/300077

BlockChain Use Cases

https://www.computerworld.com.au/article/633059/6-use-cases-blockchain-security/

https://blog.capterra.com/benefits-of-blockchain-cybersecurity/

https://www.apriorit.com/dev-blog/462-blockchain-cybersecurity-pros-cons

https://www.databreachtoday.com/blockchain-use-cases-in-cybersecurity-a-11368

https://coincentral.com/blockchain-applied-cybersecurity/

https://www.openaccessgovernment.org/use-cases-for-blockchain-in-security/42159/(6   usecase   in cyber security)

https://www2.deloitte.com/content/dam/Deloitte/us/Documents/financial-services/us-blockchain-and-cyber-security-lets-discuss.pdf(network access,right to be forgotten)

https://www.infosecurity-magazine.com/next-gen-infosec/blockchain-cybersecurity/

https://www.business.com/articles/blockchain-digital-marketing/

https://yourstory.com/2018/08/blockchain-technology-impact-digital-marketing/

https://rampedup.us/blockchain-digital-marketing/

https://curatti.com/6-ways-blockchain-help-digital-marketing/

https://qz.com/947064/sweden-is-turning-a-blockchain-powered-land-registry-into-a-reality/

https://chromaway.com/papers/Blockchain_Landregistry_Report_2017.pdf

https://chromaway.com/papers/A-blockchain-based-property-registry.pdf

https://www.coindesk.com/blockchain-land-registry-solution-seeking-problem/

https://cryptodigestnews.com/how-blockchain-is-revolutionizing-finance-9bcdb3943c06

http://newmetaverse.org/white-paper/Metaverse-digital-identity-white-paper-v1.0-EN.pdf

https://www.linkedin.com/pulse/top-30-financial-services-blockchain-use-cases-its-just-ron-shulkin

https://www2.deloitte.com/nl/nl/pages/financial-services/articles/1-blockchain-speeding-up-and-simplifying-cross-border-payments.html

https://www.investopedia.com/terms/f/fiatmoney.asp

https://developer.ibm.com/patterns/customer-loyalty-program-with-blockchain/

https://www.ipc.com/solutions/connecting-the-global-financial-community/single-source-for-private-secure-communications/financial-markets-network/

https://www.oliverwyman.com/content/dam/oliver-wyman/global/en/2016/feb/BlockChain-In-Capital-Markets.pdf

Acronyms:

- BTC   Bitcoin
- CA   Central Authority
- CPU   Central Processing Unit
- DAO   Decentralized Autonomous Organization
- DDoS   Distributed Denial of Service attack
- DID   Digital Identity
- DNS   Domain Name System
- DPOS   Delegated Proof of Stake
- ECDSA   Elliptic Curve Digital Signature Algorithm
- ICO   Initial Coin Offering
- IP   Internet Protocol
- LSK   Lisk
- NaaS   Network-as-a-Service
- NEX   NEO Exchange
- P2P   Peer-to-Peer
- P2PKH   Pay-to-Public-Key-Hash
- PII   Personally Identifiable Information
- POI   Proof of Importance
- POS   Proof of stake
- POW   Proof of Work
- QA   Quality Assurance
- SDEX   Stellar Decentralized Exchange
- SDLC   Software Development LifeCycle
- SQL   Structured Query Language
- SSL   Secure Sockets Layer

About Our Products

Other Network & Security related products from IPSpecialist LTD are:

- CCNA Routing & Switching Technology Workbook
- CCNA Security Technology Workbook
- CCNA Service Provider Technology Workbook
- CCDA Technology Workbook
- CCDP Technology Workbook
- CCNP Route Technology Workbook
- CCNP Switch Technology Workbook
- CCNP Troubleshoot Technology Workbook
- CCNP Security SENSS Technology Workbook
- CCNP Security SIMOS Technology Workbook
- CCNP Security SITCS Technology Workbook
- CCNP Security SISAS Technology Workbook
- CompTIA Network+ Technology Workbook
- CompTIA Security+ Technology Workbook
- EC-Council CEH v10 Technology Workbook
- Certified Blockchain Expert v2 Technology Workbook

Upcoming products are:

- CCNA CyberOps SECOPS Technology Workbook
- Certified Cloud Security Professional (CCSP) Technology Workbook
- Certified Application Security Engineer (Java) Technology Workbook
- Certified Application Security Engineer (.Net) Technology Workbook
- Certified Information Security Manager Technology Workbook
- Certified Information Systems Auditor Technology Workbook

Note from the Author:

Reviews are gold to authors! If you have enjoyed this book and helped you along certification, would you consider rating it and reviewing it?

Link to Product Page: